DREAMS

A C. G. JUNG FOUNDATION BOOK
Published in Association with Daimon Verlag, Einsiedeln, Switzerland

The C. G. Jung Foundation for Analytical Psychology is dedicated to helping men and women grow in conscious awareness of the psychological realities in themselves and society, find healing and meaning in their lives and greater depth in their relationships, and live in response to their discovered sense of purpose. It welcomes the public to attend its lectures, seminars, films, symposia, and workshops and offers a wide selection of books for sale through its bookstore. The Foundation also publishes *Quadrant,* a semiannual journal, and books on Analytical Psychology and related subjects. For information about Foundation programs or membership, please write to the C. G. Jung Foundation, 28 East 39th Street, New York, NY 10016.

DREAMS

MARIE-LOUISE
VON FRANZ

Foreword by Robert Hinshaw

SHAMBHALA
Boston & London
1998

SHAMBHALA PUBLICATIONS, INC.
Horticultural Hall
300 Massachusetts Avenue
Boston, Massachusetts 02115
http://www.shambhala.com

9 8 7 6 5 4 3 2 1

First Paperback Edition

Printed in the United States of America
⊛ This edition is printed on acid-free paper that meets the American National Standards Institute Z39.48 Standard.
Distributed in the United States by Random House, Inc.; in Canada by Random House of Canada Ltd.; and in the United Kingdom by the Random Century Group.

The Library of Congress catalogues the hardcover edition of this book as follows:

Franz, Marie-Louise von, 1915–
   [Träume. English]
   Dreams / Marie-Louise Von Franz: foreword by Robert Hinshaw.—1st ed. p. cm. Translation of: Träume. "A C. G. Jung Foundation book"— Includes bibliographical references.
   ISBN 0-87773-901-3
   ISBN 1-57062-035-0 (pbk.)
     1. Dreams—History. 2. Dreams—Case studies. 3. Psycho-analysis. 4. Jung, C. G. (Carl Gustav), 1875–1961. I. Title.
BF1078.F6514 1990   90-55063
154.6'3—dc20   CIP

CONTENTS

FOREWORD

Marie-Louise von Franz is one of the last of the close circle of C. G. Jung's associates still alive today. She collaborated with Jung from 1934 until his death and subsequently became an internationally respected authority in her own right. Her numerous published works on psychological subjects and a variety of interviews conducted in recent years reveal her extraordinarily far-ranging experience and lively wit. The seventy-six-year-old analyst has also distinguished herself as an outstanding lecturer and written dozens of papers for journals, anthologies, and congresses. Unfortunately, however, many of these articles and lecture manuscripts from years past have dropped out of sight; journals and proceedings go out of print and lecture notes are usually not accessible anyway.

The present volume is the first in a series of collections intended to assemble all such material into various thematic categories and make it available in book form to interested readers. Each volume will be devoted to a general theme, such as dreams, psyche and matter, and psychotherapy.

The theme of this first volume of the series, which was published in German in 1985 on the occasion of the author's seventieth birthday, is dreams. In the first two chapters, Marie-

Louise von Franz offers general explanations of the nature of dreams and the roles they can play in the course of analysis. In the first, which originally appeared as a paper in the *Schleswig-Holsteinisches Ärzteblatt* (1973), she addresses the question of the development of self-knowledge, which can accompany an attitude of taking dreams seriously. The next chapter describes the way in which Jung concerned himself with his dreams and points out fateful ways in which they were intertwined with the course of his life.

In the second part of this book, dreams of historical personages, philosophers, and politicians are recorded and interpreted. Some of these papers are based on lectures given by Marie-Louise von Franz many years ago at the C. G. Jung Institute in Zurich ("The Dream of Socrates," "The Dream of Themistocles and Hannibal," and "The Dreams of the Mother of Bernard of Clairvaux and the Mother of Saint Augustine"). The detailed chapter on a dream of Descartes originally appeared in a volume in the series "Studies in Jungian Thought" (Northwestern, 1968) which is long out of print. This section of *Dreams* is informative, not only psychologically, but also from historical, religious, and philosophical points of view. Connections are revealed between the personal and family histories of the dreamers and individual and collective mores of their times. This greater perspective pervades all of the author's work and provides fascinating insights, as the reader will be experiencing throughout this collection.

It should be emphasized that the various papers gathered for this volume were not originally written as chapters in a book. With this in mind, we have placed papers with a more general content at the beginning, followed by those lectures that were specifically addressed to analysts in training. As an aid to readers not familiar with Jungian psychology, a glossary is included that provides explanations of some of the more frequently used terms.

We are grateful to Marie-Louise von Franz, who revised her papers for publication in book form in spite of debilitating illness; to Lela Fischli for her tireless editing; and to Dr. René

Malamud, whose initiative and generous support made this volume possible.

Robert Hinshaw
Daimon Verlag
Einsiedeln, Switzerland

DREAMS

The
Hidden
Source of
Self-Knowledge

Translated by Emmanuel Xipolitas Kennedy and Vernon Brooks

The Delphic expression *gnothi sauton* ("Know thyself"), attributed to Pythagoras, has a long history in the Western world. It became famous through the teachings of Socrates and Plato, and consequently the search to acquire self-knowledge was, from that time on, more a concern of philosophy than of religion. In the religions, Western man made greater efforts toward gaining insight into the nature and meaning of the world as a whole and toward redemption from suffering than he did for *empirical insight into his own nature.* In the history of philosophy, on the other hand, we see that thinkers since Plato have concentrated more on an understanding of conscious thinking than on the *elucidation of the human being as a whole.* In the history of philosophy, it was especially the introverted thinkers who attempted, as it were, to dig reflectively into the inner background of their mental processes in a passionate search for their origins. Saint Augustine, Descartes, and Kant are instructive examples of this line of thought. All those who dug deep enough into the background of consciousness reached, in one form or another, something irrational which they usually designated with the name of "God."

On the other hand, an objective psychology in the form of

impersonal experimental observation of the human psyche began with Aristotle and led to various theories about man's so-called *pathē*, emotions, affects, and so on, as well as about his social drives. The result of this direction in the investigation of human nature can be seen in contemporary behaviorism in its many diverse gradations.

All these efforts to account for human nature have unearthed much that is valuable. But time and again we are amazed that in the process it is especially *the* source of self-knowledge which has been very little taken into consideration, or in most cases not at all, and which today we regard as the most valuable treasury of information about ourselves: *the unconscious, especially in its manifestation in dreams.* Sigmund Freud, as we know, called the dream the *via regia* ("the royal road") to the unconscious and used the dreams of his patients to help them become conscious of their repressed sexual strivings, the repression of which, according to his theory, determined the nature of all neurotic disturbances. Dreams, in his view, contain, in concealed form, allusions to instinctual desires which might as well have been conscious and which Freud believed he had "explained" (in the sense of "explaining away") in terms of his system. Jung, on the other hand, did not accept Freud's theory but retained the way of looking at dreams which he had adopted from his early studies of them, namely that they contain *something essentially unknown* which emerges creatively from the unconscious background and which must be examined anew, experimentally and objectively, in each individual case, as far as possible without preconceptions.

To this day the dream has remained an unexplained life phenomenon, having its roots deep in the physiological life processes. It is a normal, universal manifestation in all of the higher animals. We all dream about four times a night, and if someone prevents our dreaming, serious psychic and somatic disturbances result. C. G. Jung provisionally identified as relatively certain facts the following aspects of the dream:[1]

The dream has two roots, one in conscious contents, impressions of the previous day, and so forth, the second in constellated contents of the unconscious. The latter consists of two categories: (1) constellations which have their source in conscious contents; (2) constellations arising from creative processes in the unconscious.

The meaning of a dream can be formulated as follows:

1. A dream represents an unconscious reaction to a conscious situation.

2. It describes a situation which has come about as the result of some conflict between consciousness and the unconscious.

3. It represents a tendency in the unconscious whose purpose is to effect a change in a conscious attitude.

4. It represents unconscious processes which have no recognizable relation to consciousness.

These processes can be somatically determined, or they can arise from creative sources in the psyche. Finally, such processes can also be based upon physical or psychic events in the environment, either past or future. Apart from so-called shock dreams (grenade shock, etc.) a dream never simply repeats a previous experience. It is usually *after* the event that one is able to recognize the relation of a dream to some physical or psychic environmental event or some future happening; such dreams are relatively rarer than those containing an unconscious reaction to a conscious situation—the representation of a conflict between consciousness and the unconscious, or a tendency directed toward a change in consciousness. The last three types of dreams describe psychic processes which are more closely related to the experiencing subject.

For our inquiry only this latter aspect of the dream is most important.

The Dream as an Expression of an Inner Drama

One can understand every dream as a drama in which we ourselves are *everything*, that is, the author, director, actors, and prompter, as well as the spectators. If one tries to understand a dream in this way, the result is a startling realization for the dreamer of what is happening in him psychically, "behind his back," so to speak. The surprise may be experienced as painful, as joyful, or as enlightening, depending on how he accepts the dream-play in consciousness. The moment of surprise lies in what Jung called the *compensatory or complementary function of the dream.* This means that the dream almost never represents something already conscious, but rather brings either contents which balance a one-sided attitude of consciousness (compensatory) or completes what is lacking in those contents of consciousness which are too narrow or are not considered sufficiently valuable (complementary). As an example of the first case we may think of someone who suffers from feelings of insecurity and inferiority and in a dream finds himself in a hero role; in the second case we may think, for instance, of someone who entertains only a superficially felt sympathy for a partner of the opposite sex and at night dreams of a passionate love scene with that person. In the latter case the dream complements the stronger emotional importance of what has been recognized consciously, an importance which had been overlooked. *The understanding of such dreams leads* eo ipso *to a change in one's conscious views of things experienced outwardly,* as well as—and this is what concerns us—a change in our view of ourselves.

Jung relates the case of a lady who was well known for her stupid prejudices and her stubborn resistance to reasoned argument. One night she dreamed that she was invited to an important social affair. Her hostess greeted her with the words, "Oh, how nice that you have come! All your friends are here already and are expecting you." The hostess then led her to a door, opened it and the dreamer stepped into—a cowshed! "The woman would not admit at first the point of a dream that struck so directly at her self-importance; but its message nevertheless went home."[2] Many outer attractions and distractions, as Jung further emphasizes, seduce us into following ways that are unsuited to our individuality. This is especially true of people who have an extraverted, mental attitude or who harbor feelings of inferiority and doubt about themselves; they are given over to those tides of life which falsify their nature. However, dreams correct these false impressions and thus lead to a realization of *what* one is, what is in accord with one's nature, or what one is not and should therefore avoid. In this way, if one takes them seriously as subjective dramas, dreams constantly provide us with new insights about ourselves. Some intuitive arts, such as horoscopy, graphology, chiromancy, phrenology, and the like, can indeed also often provide surprising bits of self-knowledge, but dreams have a great advantage over these techniques in that they give us a dynamic, continuous self-diagnosis and also clarify smaller fluctuations and momentary erroneous attitudes or specific modes of reaction. For instance, a person can, in principle, be modest, never overvaluing himself, but can become momentarily inflated as the result of some success. A dream will correct this immediately and in doing so will inform the dreamer not only that he or she may, as a general rule, be such-and-such, but that "yesterday in connection with that matter, you were on the wrong track in such-and-such a way." Through constantly taking dreams into consideration something is produced which resembles a continuous dialogue of the conscious ego with the irrational background of the personality, a dialogue by means of which the ego is constantly revealed from the other side, as if there were a mirror, as it were, in which the dreamer can examine his own nature.

Who "Composes" a Series of Dream Images?

Now we will consider the great wonder, the quite amazing fact which lies behind every dream phenomenon examined in this way: *Who or what is this miraculous something that composes a series of dream images?* Who, for instance, is the spirit so full of good humor that created in that woman the scene with the cowshed? In general, who or what looks at us more clearly and relentlessly than one's best friend or enemy could ever do? It must be a being of the most superior intelligence—judging from the depth and cleverness of dreams. But is it a being at all? Does it have a personality or is it something more like an object, a light or the surface of a mirror? In *Memories, Dreams, Reflections* Jung calls this something "personality No. 2." He experienced it first as a personal or at least a half-personified being. "There was always, deep in the background, the feeling that something other than myself was involved. It was as though a breath of the great world of stars and endless space had touched me, or as if a spirit had invisibly entered the room—the spirit of one who had long been dead and yet was perpetually present in timelessness until far into the future."[3] This being has something to do with the "creation of dreams," "a spirit who could hold his own against the world of darkness." It was a kind of autonomous personality but did not have "any definite individuality. . . . The only distinct feature about this spirit was his historical character, his extension in time, or rather, his timelessness."[4]

Personality No. 2 is the *collective unconscious,* which Jung also later called the "objective psyche," for it is experienced as not belonging to us. (In the historical past such phenomena were looked upon as "spirit powers.") It is a "something" which is experienced by the subject ego as its opposite, like an eye, so to speak, which observes one from the depths of the soul. In his *Philosophia meditativa,* Gerhard Dorn, a follower of Paracelsus, has given a most illuminating description in many respects of this experience of the objective psyche and of the personality transformation resulting from this experience. In his view, the alchemical *opus* is based on an act of self-knowledge. This self-knowledge, however, is not what the ego thinks about itself, but something quite different. Dorn says, "But no man can truly know himself unless first he see and know by zealous meditation . . . *what* rather than *who* he is, on whom he depends, and whose he is, and to what end he was made and created, and by whom and through whom."[5]

With the emphasis on "what" (instead of "who") Dorn stresses a nonsubjective real partner which he seeks in his meditation and in his self-knowledge, and by this he means nothing other than the image of God embedded within the soul of man. Whoever observes this and frees his mind from all worldly cares and distractions, "little by little and from day to day will perceive with his mental eyes and with the greatest joy some sparks of divine illumination."[6] Whoever in this way recognizes God in himself will also recognize his brother. Jung called this inner center, which Dorn equates with the god-image, the *Self.* In Paracelsus's view, man learns about this inner light through his dreams: "As the light of nature cannot speak, it buildeth shapes in sleep from the power of the word."[7]

Other alchemists compared this inner light with the eyes of a fish—or with a single fish eye—which begin to shine out of the cooked *prima materia.* Nicholas Flamel, an alchemist of the seventeenth century, equated this motif with the eyes of God mentioned in Zechariah 4:10: "those seven . . . are the eyes of the Lord that run to and fro through the whole earth." (See also Zechariah 3:9: "upon one stone shall be seven eyes," etc.)[8]

The collective unconscious and its contents express themselves through dreams, and each time we succeed in understanding a dream and in morally assimilating its message we "begin to see (the light)"—hence the eye motif! One sees oneself for a moment through the eyes of another, of something objective which views one from the outside, as it were. Paracelsus, Dorn, and many others then describe many eyes gradually growing together into *one* great light; this single light is for them the light of Nature and at the same time comes from God. Dorn says, for instance, "For the life, the light of man, shineth in us, albeit dimly, and as though in darkness. It is not to be extracted from us, yet it is in us and not of us, but of Him to Whom it belongs, Who deigns to make us his dwelling place. . . . He has implanted that light in us that we may see in *its* light . . . *the* light. . . . Thus truth is to be sought not in ourselves, but in the image of God which is within us."[9] This inner light, according to Paracelsus, "is that which giveth faith."[10] I understand 1 Corinthians 13:12 ("Now I know in part, but then shall I know even as also I am known") as an allusion to this experience. This eye first sees us and through it we then see God.

The Inner Eye

The equation of this light or fish's eye that exists in man's unconscious with the eye of God, which looks at us from within and in whose light there lies at the same time the only nonsubjective source of self-knowledge, is a widespread archetypal image.[11] It is described as a bodiless inner eye in the human being, surrounded by light, or is itself a light.[12] Plato, and many Christian mystics as well, call it the eye of the soul.[13] Others have called it the eye of intelligence, of the intuition of faith, of simplemindedness, etc. Only through this eye can man see himself and the nature of God, which itself is an eye. Synesius of Cyrene (Hymn 3) even speaks of God as the "eye of yourself,"[14] and insofar as man opens his inner eye he participates in God's light. When man closes his physical eyes in sleep his soul "sees" the truth in a dream. Aeschylus says that "when we sleep the soul is lit up completely by many eyes; with them we can see everything that we could not see in the daytime."[15] And a Hermetic philosopher declares, "The sleep of my body created that illumination of the soul; my closed eyes saw the truth."[16]

This eye which looks at us from within has to do with what we usually call conscience. A poem by Victor Hugo describes this in an incomparably impressive way.[17] When Cain killed his brother Abel, he fled from God. Together with his family he rested near a mountain but could not sleep. "He saw an eye, wide open in the darkness, staring at him in the dark." "I am still too close," he called out, trembling, and continued his flight. He made haste for thirty days and thirty nights until he reached the seashore, but when he settled there he saw the eye in the heavens once again. Shouting, he pleaded with his family to hide him from God, to pitch a tent for him; still Cain saw the eye. Finally, at his request, his family dug a deep grave for him in the earth; he sat on a small stool down inside the grave and his family pushed a tombstone over him. However, when the grave was closed and he was sitting in the dark, "the eye was in the grave and looked at Cain" ("L'oeil était dans la tombe et regardait Cain"). This eye is not always perceived to be God's eye; it can also be the "dark god" who stares at us in this way. A bishop—so goes a legend from St. Gallen—once broke his fast before Easter. A beggar came to him to ask for help. When the bishop touched the beggar he discovered a huge eye on the man's breast. Terrified, he crossed himself and at that moment the Devil (for the beggar was the Devil) dissolved in smoke and as he disappeared called out, "This eye observed you closely when you were eating meat during Lent!" Many gods and demons of various mythological culture groups have such a large eye on their breast; thus they see everything that takes place on earth.[18] This motif points to the fact—which we can observe time and again in the analysis of the dreams of patients—that the unconscious in us often seems to possess a knowledge of things which were previously inexplicable and which, seen *rationally,* we cannot know. Such terms as "telepathy" do not explain the phenomenon. But we are able to recognize every day that dreams speak to people of things which they obviously cannot know. The unconscious seems to have something like a diffuse intuitive knowledge which reaches into our surroundings, and which Jung called "absolute knowledge" (because it is detached from consciousness) or the "luminosity" of the unconscious.

Sometimes we experience the unconscious as though we were being actively and uncannily observed by a personified being, at other times rather as if we were observed in a nonpersonified background, in a mirror, which unintentionally simply reflects our nature. The eye itself, in which, as we know, we can also see ourselves reflected, sometimes acts rather impersonally, not like the eye of another living being. Jung says, therefore, that the eye motif or mandala motif represents *a reflection of insight into ourselves.*

What this means practically can best be illustrated with a dream example which Jung mentions in *Man and His Symbols.*[19] A very cautious, introverted youth dreamed that he and two other young men are riding on horseback across a wide field. The dreamer is in the lead, and they jump over a ditch full of water. The two companions fall into the ditch, but the dreamer manages to jump across unhurt. The exact same dream was also dreamed by an old man who was ill in a hospital and who, due to his much too enterprising spirit, gave his doctor and nurses a great deal of trouble. In the first case, it is more appropriate to understand the dream as trying to encourage the hesitant young man to take the lead and dare to do something; in the second case, the dream shows the old man what he still does but actually should no longer be doing at his age.

Strictly speaking, however, these are conclusions which *we* draw from the dream image; the image itself does not encourage nor does it warn, it simply represents a psychic fact—as impersonally as a mirror. In that way dreams are simply like nature. If a doctor finds sugar in the urine of a patient, nature does not choose to comment on this in any way; the doctor must draw the conclusion that there is diabetes and prescribe the diet and advise the patient to exercise discipline in order to keep the diet—otherwise the doctor cannot help him. This is also how it is with dreams. They show us a psychic fact; it is up to *us* to interpret it correctly and draw the moral conclusions.

Sometimes, however, we find the opposite, namely that a dream gives advice like a well-meaning *person*. I had a rich elderly woman analysand who had been alcoholic and had given up drinking. But the neurotic problems which lay behind her alcoholism, especially a general demoralization and slovenliness, still had to be worked out. Once she dreamed that a voice told her, "You need a breakfast corset." I asked her in great detail what time she ate breakfast, what kind of corset she wore, when she put it on, etc. I discovered then that out of vanity she wore a very tight corset but never put it on in the morning; rather, she breakfasted in her dressing gown, then dawdled around the apartment in her negligée the rest of the morning and put her corset on around noon. Only then did her day actually begin. After this information, the dream no longer needed interpretation; we both laughed heartily. Now and then, however, I would ask her, "How is it going with the breakfast corset?"

In view of these facts, it is understandable that the unconscious or the dream spirit that creates the dreams appears to us at times rather like a conscious being full of intentions and at other times rather like an impersonal mirror. The *eye motif* lies, as it were, in the middle; it is both something *personal* and at the same time a *mirror*. The fact that almost all the religions of the earth include a partly personified god-image or a non-personified world order (such as the Chinese Tao) and the fact also that in historical periods of the same culture the emphasis at some times was more on a personal god-image and at other times on an impersonal world principle—these facts are probably connected with the above experiences. In the Judeo-Christian tradition we have a predominantly personal god-image, but the definition of God as "an intelligible sphere whose center is everywhere and whose circumference is nowhere" has played a paramount role in the thinking of many great Western theologians, mystics, and philosophers. In this connection I would like to refer the reader to Dietrich Mahnke's excellent book, *Unendliche Sphäre und Allmittelpunkt* (Darmstadt, 1966).

The appearance of a personified inner being, that is, a personified god-image, looking at or speaking to us, supports the development of *feeling* and of ethical behavior—in the case of that woman it was indeed a question of a moral problem. The image of an impersonal soul-center or cosmic psychograph, as Giuseppe Tucci calls the mandala, satisfies rather the *knowledge* or intuition of man as an image of a great divine unified world-center, or of a supra-personal meaning behind the world of appearances. However, one must not become excited by supposing that this provides any proof concerning the existence of God; it is rather a question of God's *images* manifesting spontaneously in the soul of man, which are therefore anthropomorphic and do not say anything definite about an ultimate metaphysical existence of the soul or of the divinity. These images are simply the only ones we can observe empirically in our daily work and whose effect on the personality of the dreamer can be recognized.

In Jungian psychotherapy we use dreams for the most part to guide the analysand to certain insights or self-knowledge, for there is no psychic healing and no progress without self-knowledge—self-knowledge, however, in the sense of recognizing *what one is* (as Gerhard Dorn describes it), not in the superficial notion which the ego has about itself or in taking over the analyst's idea about one's self. This is also the reason that, in actual practice, we do not give the analysand a diagnosis but, for the most part, say only, "Let us see how your own soul views your situation"—namely what the dreams say. In this way any personal interference of the analyst in the life of the analysand is restricted, at least as much as possible. I once had an analysand who had to give up alcohol, which he did bravely for a couple of months. Then he said to me, "Listen, don't you think I could dare now to have *one* glass of beer in the evening at the Sternen Hotel with Betty? Just *one* glass? I am always so lost in the evenings, so lonely." Although I knew this was not advisable, I just said, "I don't know; I don't want to be your governess. Try it and we will see how the unconscious reacts." He did this, drank his glass of beer and went home. That night he dreamed of driving his car up a mountain, all the way to the top, but when he got there he did not brake properly and the car rolled backward all the way down the mountain until he was back where he started. I merely said, smiling, "Tableau!" He immediately realized that "only *one* glass of beer" would not work. His "inner eye" had seen the situation of the previous evening in that way and not in any other.

The Self: Soul-Center in the Unconscious

Jung has chosen the term *Self* for the soul-center in the unconscious, borrowing it from East Indian philosophy. Although this can lead to misunderstanding the Self to be the same as the ego, it is important that what is implied is its relationship with the human individual, for that is how we find it represented in dreams.

The son of a parson had a nightmare which was repeated throughout his life but which was modified in the course of time. In this dream he was going through a vast desert at night when he heard some footsteps behind him. Fearful, he walked faster; the steps quickened too. He began to run, the horrible "something" following behind him. He reached the edge of a deep abyss and had to stop. Looking down, far, far below, down thousands of miles, he saw the burning fires of hell. He looked back and saw in the dark behind him a vaguely demonic face.

Later he had exactly the same dream except that instead of a demon he saw the face of God. Then when he was about fifty years old he dreamed the dream once again. However, this time his panic fear drove him over the edge of the abyss. As he fell, thousands of quadrangular paper sheets floated down from above and on every sheet was a drawing in black and white of a different mandala. The little sheets then merged into a kind of floor which, by providing a solid plane half-way down, prevented him from falling all the way into hell. He looked back, up to the edge of the abyss; there he saw *his own face!*

The lengthy naves of our churches, far from the intersecting aisles and from the altar, reflect the fact, as Jung once mentioned in a letter, that in our culture man is experienced as being far away from God; God is the "wholly other" (Barth) and we forget that He is simultaneously the most intimately known in our innermost soul. This paradox is better known to East Indians; for them the *atman-purusha,* the *Self,* is the innermost nucleus of the soul of the individual *and* at the same time the cosmic, divine All-Spirit. The dreamer of the repeated nightmare was also educated in Western views of God as the "wholly other"—hence his dream calls his attention to the opposite aspect.

I tried to explain above what is meant by interpreting a dream on the subjective level, that is, as an *inner drama* in which all objects and figures represent unknown aspects of the dreamer. So, when interpreting dreams we ask the dreamer simply to provide us with a vivid, feeling-toned image of the way a person he meets in a dream appears to him. Then we "feed" the same information "back" to the dreamer. What he says about X, of whom he dreamed, will be an image of something in the dreamer himself.

The unconscious seems to possess a peculiar talent for using complicated images of experience to convey something unknown to consciousness. But we can observe this not only through dreams; in waking states, too, we often see in other people elements of an impossibly wide-ranging nature which are really present in ourselves; sometimes this goes as far as a complete distortion of the image of the other person. *This is the familiar phenomenon of projection, which Jung defines as an unintentional transfer of a part of the psyche which belongs to the subject onto an outer object.* It is the well-known business of the beam in our eye which we do not see. Then, however, practical problems arise.

Projection

We probably project all the time, in everything we do; in other words, in addition to those other impressions which are conveyed by the senses, there are always psychosomatic influences from within, so that we have a general impression of our experiences; Gestalt psychology demonstrates this in many individual cases. Therefore we must either widen our concept of projection to such an extent that, like the East Indians, we look upon everything as projection; or we must draw a line between what we will refer to as projection and what is a relatively objective statement concerning outer objects. Jung suggested that the concept of projection be applied only where there is *a serious disturbance of adaptation,* that is to say, where either the person who is doing the projecting or all those in his immediate vicinity unanimously reject the statement in question. For the usual mixture of subjectivity in our image of reality, a mixture which is limitless, Jung uses the expression *archaic identity, archaic* because this was man's original condition, namely one in which he saw all psychic processes in an "outside"—his good and evil thoughts as spirits, his affects as gods (Ares, Cupid), and so on. Only gradually were certain psychic processes, which were visualized before as exclusively "outside," understood as processes within the experiencing subject himself, as for instance when the Stoic philosophers began to interpret the goddess Athena as insight, Ares as aggressive passion, Aphrodite as erotic desire; this, so to speak, was the beginning of an "incarnation" of the gods in man.

How far such a process can go—a process, that is, of an

increasing development of consciousness—is therefore not easy to foresee. We still know pitifully little about objective man, as Jung emphasized time and again. In spite of being disturbing and socially dangerous, projections also have a meaning; for it is apparently only through projections that we can make ourselves conscious of certain unconscious processes. Through projections there arise, first of all, those fascinations, affects, entanglements which then force us to reflect on ourselves. There is *no becoming conscious without the fires of emotion and suffering.* The disturbance of adaptation which is closely linked with every projection leads, if all goes well, to reflection (if it goes badly it leads to homicide and murder). *Re-flexio,* however, means that the image which has been "radiated" outward onto another object is "bent back" and returns to oneself. It is just because the symbol of the mirror has to do psychologically with the phenomenon of projection that it has, mythologically, such an enormous magical significance. In a mirror one can recognize oneself or see a projection. An old Scottish shepherd who lived a secluded life found a pocket mirror one day which a tourist had lost. He had never seen such a thing before. Time after time he looked at it, was amazed, shook his head, then took it home with him. His wife watched with increasing jealousy as, time and again, he furtively drew something out of his pocket, looked at it, smiled, put it back. When he was away one day she quickly took the mirror out of his coat pocket. Looking at it, she cried, "Aha! So *this* is the old witch he is running after now!"

That "constant flow of projections"—that is to say, that activity in which the subjective intrapsychic elements in our experience of the outer world does *not* disturb adaptation— Jung, as mentioned above, has called *archaic identity,* from which all genuine, true knowledge originates, for it is based on an instinctual, mystic participation with all things and all other people. "It is as if the 'eyes of the background,' " as Jung describes it, "do the seeing in an impersonal act of perception."[20] *These* eyes see accurately. Why then do all those projections which disturb adaptation and which must be corrected through conscious insight also come from the same unconscious background? This is probably connected with what we call the *dissociability* of the psyche. Our entire psyche seems to consist of separate complexes which gather together into what one could call the psychic individuality, just as the Mendelian units of our hereditary factors together form a unity.

We can clearly see in a small child, who still possesses a very labile ego-consciousness, how loosely the separate complexes live with each other in the moods which change like lightning and by means of which the youngster can switch from "loving child" to "devil" and vice versa, one moment completely affectionate, the next minute utterly engrossed in his play, one moment in deep despair, two minutes later joyful again, sucking a candy. These fluctuations decrease slowly as the conscious ego gradually builds itself up, but then the ego often experiences collisions of the individual complex-impulses within and must then learn to endure and control them. Once, when I was nine, I wanted to draw a picture of my dog whom I loved passionately, but he wouldn't sit still. I was furious so I smacked him and shouted at him. I will never forget that dog's innocent, offended look! I did not hit him again, but when I sat down to finish my drawing I felt clearly within me how the fury of my impatience and my love for the dog clashed painfully together. Jung conjectured once that ego consciousness first develops from collisions of the small child with the outer world and later from collisions of the growing ego with the impulses from its own inner world (as in the example of my fury with my dog). The "parliament of instincts," as Konrad Lorenz would have called it, is not a peaceful organization within us; it is rather violent in there, and the President—the ego—often has difficulty asserting himself. From a practical point of view we can observe that whenever a complex becomes autonomous, then there always arise projections which disturb adaptation and blur the "mirror of the inner truth."

People in one's immediate neighborhood experience our projections as emotional exaggerations. Personally, I listen almost unconsciously to the tone in which analysands speak about their marital partner, their friends and enemies, and I have discovered that I simply "switch over" whenever a certain undertone of hysterical exaggeration is heard together with the rest of the patient's statement. Then one can no longer quite believe what is being said, but instead listens to an interesting (unconscious) self-presentation of the analysand. If one succeeds in that moment in relating such an outburst to a dream motif which pictures the statements figuratively, then there is often a good chance that the other will see that all that he has described so enthusiastically or so angrily is really in himself. The withdrawal of a projection, however, is almost always a moral shock. People with weak egos are often unable to tolerate this and resist violently. Jung once compared the ego with a person who navigates his sturdy or flimsy boat on the sea of the unconscious. He hauls fish (the contents of the unconscious) into his boat, but he cannot fill the boat (i.e., integrate unconscious contents) with more fish than the size of the boat allows; if he takes in too many the boat sinks. That is why the elucidation and the withdrawal of projections is a critical matter. Schizoid and hysterical personalities can usually take only a little. With primitive people who have a weak ego, it is also advisable to leave projections unexplained. It has been my experience that then the older, more historical ways of dealing with autonomous complexes work better, namely that one refers to them as "spirits" which do not belong to the individual and thus one helps the analysand to resist such a "spirit" through some ritual or magic practice. This means that one takes literally what has been preserved as a figure of speech: "The devil has gotten into him" or that being in love is a "bewitchment." However, any decisions about these inner moral insights will be made *not by the ego* and *not by the analyst* but *by the Self*. So we are in fact just as the Self sees us with its inner eyes which are always open, and all our own efforts toward self-knowledge must get to this point before any inner peace is possible.

However, the mandala (as the principle image of the Self) has a strict mathematical order—like the symbol of the mirror—for, seen from a physical point of view, only those material surfaces which have no distortions, whose molecules are well-arranged, are capable of reflection. Therefore, it would appear as though the truth of one's own being were reflected there, in the innermost core of the soul—from *there* come our dreams, which show us how we really are, whereas the distorting projections come from partial complexes which have made themselves autonomous. This is why Zen masters tell their pupils, time after time, that they should free their "inner mirror" (Buddha-mind) of dust.

As long as we live, our reflection tries to penetrate into the deeper secrets of our innermost being, but what urges us to this is the Self itself, for which we search. It searches for itself in us. It seems to me that it is this secret to which a dream of Jung points, which he had after a severe illness in 1944, and which he relates in his memoirs. In this dream he is walking through a sunny, hilly landscape when he comes to a small wayside chapel. "The door was ajar, and I went in. To my surprise there was no image of the Virgin on the altar, and no crucifix either, but only a wonderful flower arrangement. But then I saw that on the floor in front of the altar, facing me, sat a yogi—in lotus posture, in deep meditation. When I looked at him more closely, I realized that he had my face. I started in profound fright, and awoke with the thought: 'Aha, so he is the one who is meditating me. He has a dream and I am it.' I knew that when he awakened, I would no longer be."[21]

The dream, Jung continues,

> is a parable: My self retires into meditation and meditates my earthly form. To put it another way: it assumed human shape in order to enter three-dimensional existence, as if someone were putting on a diver's suit in order to dive into the sea. When it renounces existence in the hereafter, the self assumes a religious posture, as the chapel in the dream shows. In earthly form it can pass through the experiences of the three-dimensional world, and by greater awareness take a further step toward realization.[22]

The figure of the yogi represents, as it were, Jung's prenatal wholeness whose meditation "projects" the empirical reality of the ego. As a rule we see these things in reverse, we discover mandalas in the products of the unconscious and express therewith our idea of wholeness. Our basis is ego-consciousness, a field of light centered upon the focal point of the ego. From that point we look out upon an enigmatic world of obscurity and do not know how far its shadowy forms are caused by our consciousness and how far they possess a reality of their own. The tendency of the dream, writes Jung,

> is to effect a reversal of the relationship between ego-consciousness and the unconscious, and to represent the unconscious as the generator of the empirical personality. This reversal suggests that in the opinion of the "Other side," our unconscious existence is the real one and our conscious world a kind of illusion, an apparent reality constructed for a specific purpose. . . . *Unconscious wholeness* therefore seems to me the *true spiritus rector* of all biological and psychic events. Here is a principle which strives for total realization—which in man's case signifies the attainment of total consciousness. Attainment of consciousness is culture in the broadest sense, and self-knowledge is therefore the heart and essence of this process. The Oriental attributes unquestionably divine significance to the self, and according to the ancient Christian view self-knowledge is the road to *knowledge of God.*[23]

You see why I have called this paper, "The Hidden Source of Self-Knowledge"; it lies within us and yet is an unfathomable secret, a complete cosmos which we have only begun to explore.

Notes

1. C. G. Jung, *Kinderträume.* Seminar given at the Eidgenössische Technische Hochschule, Zurich, 1936/37, unpublished, pp. 6–7.
2. C. G. Jung, ed., *Man and His Symbols* (New York: Doubleday, 1964), p. 49.
3. C. G. Jung, *Memories, Dreams, Reflections,* ed. Aniela Jaffé, trans. Richard and Clara Winston (New York: Random House, 1989), p. 66.

4. Ibid., pp. 89–90.
5. Cited in C. G. Jung, *Mysterium Coniunctionis*, *CW* 14, par. 684.
6. Ibid., par. 685.
7. Cited in C. G. Jung, "On the Nature of the Psyche," *CW* 8, par. 391. *Liber de caducis*, Huser, vol. 4, p. 274; or Sudhoff, vol. 7, p. 224.
8. Cf. Jung, "On the Nature of the Psyche," par. 394.
9. Cited ibid., par. 389.
10. Cited ibid., par. 390.
11. Ibid., par. 394.
12. Cf. Waldemar Deonna, *Le symbolisme de l'oeil* (Paris, 1965), pp. 46ff.
13. Ibid., p. 47n.
14. Ibid., p. 49.
15. *The Eumenides*, verses 104–105.
16. Deonna, p. 51.
17. "La conscience." Cf. Henri Sensine, *Chiréstomathie française du XIX siècle* (Lausanne, 1899), pp. 99f. Originally from *La légende des siècles*.
18. Cf. Deonna, pp. 64–65.
19. P. 66.
20. Jung, *Memories, Dreams, Reflections*, p. 50.
21. Ibid., p. 323.
22. Ibid., pp. 323–324.
23. Ibid., pp. 324–325; italics added.

HOW C. G. JUNG LIVED with His DREAMS

Translated by Emmanuel Xipolitas Kennedy and Vernon Brooks

Jung was a good dreamer, as he remarks in his memoirs. Throughout his life he had a great number of impressive and symbolically profound dreams which he observed, wrote down, and kept in mind. Near the end of his life he decided to make some of these deeper dreams known to the public, for they were obviously related to his creative work. His dreams were his real self and the source of everything he did and everything he wrote; for him they represented the essence of his life.

"In the end," he said, "the only events in my life worth telling are those when the imperishable world irrupted into this transitory one. That is why I speak chiefly of inner experiences, amongst which I include my dreams and visions. These form the *prima materia* of my scientific work. They were the fiery magma out of which the stone that had to be worked was crystallized."[1] "I arrived early at the insight that when no answer comes from within to the problems and complexities of life, they ultimately mean very little."[2]

The earliest dream which Jung could recall was from his third or fourth year and, as is the case with the earliest dream which most people can recall, revealed the basic structure of his being and his fate. It was as follows:

The vicarage [where he grew up as a child] stood quite alone near Laufen castle, and there was a big meadow stretching back from the sexton's farm. In the dream I was in this meadow. Suddenly I discovered a dark, rectangular, stone-lined hole in the ground. . . . I ran forward curiously and peered down into it. Then I saw a stone stairway leading down. Hesitantly and fearfully, I descended. At the bottom was a doorway with a round arch, closed off by a green curtain. It was a big, heavy curtain . . . and it looked very sumptuous. Curious to see what might be hidden behind, I pushed it aside. I saw before me in the dim light a rectangular chamber about thirty feet long. The ceiling was arched and of hewn stone. The floor was laid with flagstones, and in the center a red carpet ran from the entrance to a low platform. On this platform stood a wonderfully rich golden throne. . . . Something was standing on it, which I thought at first was a tree trunk. . . . It was a huge thing, reaching almost to the ceiling. But it was of a curious composition: it was made of skin and naked flesh, and on top there was something like a rounded head with no face and no hair. On the very top of the head was a single eye, gazing motionlessly upward.

It was fairly light in the room, although there were no windows and no apparent source of light. Above the head, however, was an aura of brightness. The thing did not move, yet I had the feeling that at any moment it might crawl off the throne like a worm and creep toward me. I was paralyzed with terror. At that moment I heard from outside and above me my mother's voice. She called out, "Yes, just look at him. That is the man-eater!" That intensified my terror still more, and I awoke sweating and scared to death.[3]

The "thing" was a ritual phallus. The term *phallus* is Greek for the male organ and is related to the word *phalos*—"bright, shining"—hence also the "aura of brightness" surrounding it in the dream; it is represented as a buried royal being. This underground structure was, as Jung writes in old age, "a subterranean God, 'not to be named,' " a counterpart, as it were, to the "loving, Christian God," which, as a child, he naturally imagined to be sitting on a throne in heaven. "Who spoke to me then?" cried Jung. "Who talked of problems far beyond my knowledge? Who brought the Above and the Below together, and laid the foundation for everything that was to fill the second half of my life with stormiest passion? Who disturbed my unadulterated harmless childhood with a heavy knowledge of maturest human life?[4] Who but that alien guest who came both from above and from below?"[5] A numbskull will speak of "chance" and "retrospective interpretation" and the like in order to belittle the dream. "Ah, these good, efficient, healthy-minded people, they always remind me of those optimistic tadpoles who bask in a puddle in the sun, in the shallowest of waters, crowded together and amiably wriggling their tails, totally unaware that the next morning the puddle will have dried up and left them stranded."[6]

In the history of religion the phallus in the grave is a well-known image of God, or of the god-image when it is in a state of transformation and psychic renewal, and at the same time it also stands for the inner man who lies buried within us, awaiting resurrection, as it were; it also symbolizes the mystery of the creative energies in the soul.

Jung's life *was* determined by his *genius* which always followed him everywhere and drove him to his creative work and also by the creative spirit of Eros, of which the phallus is a symbol. All of the central ideas in Jung's entire life work revolve around the problem of the god-image and of the experience of God, upon which the existence of every culture group depends and which, in our time, so urgently needs transformation and renewal. When the basic religious ideas of a culture are no longer creatively effective in the soul of its people, then, as the historian Arnold Toynbee has convincingly put it, that culture is doomed to extinction.

Jung did not interpret his dreams by immediately forming a clear idea of what they meant; instead, he carried them around within himself, lived with them inwardly, as it were, and asked questions of them. If he came across something in a book or in an outer experience which reminded him of a dream image, he would add it to that image, so to speak, so that a fabric of ideas developed, with a constantly increasing richness. So when, fifty years after this childhood dream, he read something about the motif of cannibalism that underlies the symbolism of the Mass, he said that it "burned into [his] eyes," meaning that he then saw another new aspect of the mysterious dream image. Later, in his work on dream interpretation, he called this weaving of ideas and experiences here and there around a dream image "amplification," by which he meant an enrichment of the dream through spontaneous ideas and related concepts.

During his first years at school Jung became more and more aware that he was actually two personalities. One, which he called "No. 1," was a normal schoolboy, son of his parents, "less intelligent, attentive, hardworking, decent and clean than many other boys." The "Other," however, was grown-up, even skeptical, remote from the world of men, but close to nature, to "all living creatures, and above all close to the night, to dreams, and to whatever 'God' worked directly in him, . . . God as a hidden, personal, and at the same time suprapersonal secret."[7] "No. 2" is what the world's religions call the "inner man," to whom God speaks and to whom He also puts terrible questions. Personality No. 2 is what modern depth psychology calls the unconscious—something in which we are all psychically contained and in which we all live, but which we really do not know; it is truly unconscious. It is so unknown to us that we cannot even say *my* unconscious; for we do not know where it begins or where it leaves off. Our dreams come from this realm. Contrary to various other schools of psychology, Jung never let himself be pushed into "explaining" this unconscious by way of a theory or a religious teaching; for him it always remained literally that which is unknown to us, of an immeasurable depth and breadth.

But the dreams which come from this unconscious are evidence of a superior intelligence. It is as if a timeless spirit spoke to us there, "as though a breath of the great world of stars and endless space" touched us, or "one who had long been dead and yet was perpetually present in timelessness until far into the future."[8] We are all close to this world spirit in childhood, but many of us forget about it as we grow older. Jung, however, could never persuade himself to forget it, although he also had to distance himself from it in order not to get caught in the dream world of childhood. He did not want to lose the "higher intelligence" which he felt to be at work in the dream. He suspected that something like a "spirit of the times" lived in No. 2, something related to the historical problems of our culture. He says, "Although we human beings have our own personal life, we are yet in large measure the representatives, the victims and promoters of a collective spirit whose years are counted in centuries. We can well think all our lives that we are following our own noses, and may never discover that we are, for the most part, supernumeraries on the stage of the world theater. . . . Thus at least a part of our being lives in the centuries,"⁹ and out of this part come the big impressive dreams, which prompt a feeling that they are concerned with more than small personal everyday problems.

Because the dream for Jung was a message from something greater, something unknown, which touches one from within, which was and always will be, it was impossible for him to create an intellectual dream theory; for him each dream had to be unraveled time and again in its uniqueness and its new meanings. Although he listened to thousands of dreams during his therapeutic practice and made every effort to interpret them, a dream always remained for him an exciting mysterious message from the creative primal source of nature. As it is for everyone, for him it was most difficult of all to interpret his own dreams.

Once, after great effort, when he had finally uncovered the meaning of a subtle dream of mine, Jung wiped his forehead and exclaimed, laughing, "You are lucky! I have no Jung to interpret *my* dreams!" He differed from Sigmund Freud in his method of understanding dreams. During the time they worked together, both he and Freud often told their dreams to each other; but once when Jung related an important dream of his to Freud, it became clear to him that he could not accept Freud's theoretical assumptions. In that dream he had de-scended the stairs in "his house" into ever deeper cellars where he discovered archaeological artifacts. Right at the bottom he found a prehistoric grave with two human skulls and broken pottery. The dream was an outline, so to speak, of his later development: he descended into deeper and deeper layers of his soul. Freud, however, preferred to understand the dream on the personal level and asked only about the skulls; he wanted Jung to look for something "murdered," that is, repressed, in his soul. Jung misled Freud with a rather poor excuse, for he felt that Freud could not have understood his interpretation.[10]

This is indicative of how much the interpretation of dreams depends on an exact agreement between the two partners. Jung suddenly felt that his dream meant *him, his* life and *his* world, and that he had to defend it against any theory derived from other presuppositions. It was for this reason that later he also allowed others the freedom which he claimed for himself; he never forced an interpretation on anyone. When it did not naturally click with the dreamer, when, in a sense, it did not produce an invigorating, liberating "Aha!" reaction in the latter, then the interpretation was not correct, or if, later on, it proved to be "right," then the dreamer was not far enough along in his development to be able to recognize it. For this reason dream interpretation for Jung always remained a dialogue between two partners with equal rights and never became for him a medical method.

The dreams of creative people are of course the most difficult to understand, for they contain suggestions for new ideas and inspirations as yet unknown to the ego. This is one reason Jung's dreams were so problematic; they often incorporated new ideas which he still had to formulate in consciousness. He once said, "Naturally, all day long I have exciting ideas and thoughts. But I take up in my work only those to which my dreams direct me." Although he entertained little hope that others might be able to understand his dreams, he was in the habit of relating them to pupils and close friends. He would "paint" them in great detail, adding all the spontaneous ideas (the so-called *associations*) to each image, and often in so doing would suddenly recognize the meaning of the dream; even naive questions of a listener would sometimes help guide him onto the right path.

Dreams which anticipate the future are also especially difficult to understand, for it is only later that one realizes their meaning. But dreams frequently *do* anticipate the future. With primitive peoples, also with the ancient Greeks and Romans and during the Middle Ages, as well as among simpler folk today, dreams are looked upon solely as information concerning future events. Hence in addition to Freud's so-called causal dream interpretation, in which one looks in dreams for past causes of the dreamer's problems—for instance, childhood experiences—Jung also called for a finalistic interpretation which recognizes inclinations directed toward a future goal—healing tendencies, for instance, in cases of psychic illness. In waking life many events appear to be suddenly motivated, whereas in the unconscious they have a long previous history. Beyond that, some dreams do seem indeed to "know" the future in some way we still do not understand. What is irritating is that so often they seem to express themselves "unclearly." If the dream spirit knows so much, why does it not convey it more clearly? Why does it speak in seemingly meaningless mosaic images, which one must decipher with great difficulty? This is also the reason many people react negatively and say, "Dreams are just bubbles." Jung was of the opinion that the unconscious, which produces dreams, does *not* know how to express its tendencies and its "knowledge" more clearly, not out of some kind of malice or because of some inhibition (as with Freud's censor theory) but rather because consciousness has an obliterating effect on the unconscious. The "illuminating" element of a dream is like candlelight which fades as soon as one switches on the electric light of ego-consciousness. This is why, when examining a dream, one must close the eyes a bit, that is, one must not proceed too strictly on an intellectual level, but must allow intuition and feeling to express themselves and, not least, a little humor too, for the dream spirit of the unconscious sometimes likes to make a joke. Jung would often laugh when someone related a dream to him which criticized the dreamer; then the latter would himself suddenly realize where the unconscious "hint" had been directed.

There is another uncertainty about dreams which often puts obstacles in the way of their interpretations. Jung understood all dreams in the first place as inner dramas in which we, the dreamers, are ourselves the actors, the scenery, and the spectators. For instance, if I am chased in a dream by a raging bull, this symbolizes an affect of my own, a wild rage in me, of which I am not conscious or not conscious enough. Jung referred to this approach as interpretation on the subjective level, because every dream image symbolizes something psychic in the dreamer, in the subject. However, although this makes possible the best and most frequently accurate interpretation, such is not always the case. Sometimes we dream of things which concern a person in our surroundings, sometimes even of things in the wider world. Thus Jung once entertained a great many doubts about a female patient, and the treatment seemed to get stuck. Then he dreamed that he saw this woman sitting up on a kind of balustrade on a tower, looking down at him in the late afternoon sunlight. He had to bend his head far back in order to see her properly. He said to himself, "If . . . I had to look up at the patient in this fashion, in reality I had probably been looking down on her."[11] When he told the woman the dream and his interpretation of it, contact between them was immediate and the treatment continued once again. Jung called this the compensating aspect of the dream, one which provides a counterbalance to one-sidedness.

When Jung dreamed of something important about someone in his immediate vicinity, he almost always told it to the person in question, often without any interpretation. The other was then free to decide for himself whether it concerned him or not. But events in more distant places sometimes also announce themselves in dreams or a waking fantasy that breaks into consciousness. In October 1913, while traveling on a train, Jung was suddenly seized by an "overpowering vision" which he relates in *Memories, Dreams, Reflections*. "I saw a monstrous flood covering all the northern and low-lying lands between the North Sea and the Alps. When it came up to Switzerland I saw that the mountains grew higher and higher to protect our country. I realized that a frightful catastrophe was in progress.

I saw the mighty yellow waves, the floating rubble of civilization, and the drowned bodies of uncounted thousands. Then the whole sea turned to blood."¹² The vision recurred in a subsequent dream, even more horrible than before. Then in the spring and early summer of 1914 he dreamed that in the middle of the summer "an Arctic cold wave descended and froze the land to ice." However, the third time the dream had a comforting resolution; in all that frigid lifelessness he saw a leaf-bearing tree, but without fruit ("my tree of life," he thought), whose leaves had been transformed by the effects of the frost into sweet grapes full of healing juices; he plucked the grapes and gave them to a large waiting crowd.¹³

At first Jung understood these dreams of his to have a personal meaning and feared that they foresaw the outbreak of a psychosis, since psychoses, as is known, are often heralded through dreams of cosmic catastrophe. One can imagine what torment and what inner distress he suffered at the time! Then, in August 1914, World War I broke out and he knew that the dreams had referred to that event. During the war he went on with his work, which he later bequeathed to mankind.

In reality he had an experience at that time which was similar to those of primitive medicine-men who, in the views of primitive people, often dream the future of the world or of their tribe and can thus warn their people in advance of coming events. There still exist today scattered in the forests of the Labrador peninsula some very poor Indians, the Naskapi, who have no tribal religion. But they believe that each of them possesses the Mistap'eo, the "Great Man in the Heart," who represents the immortal nucleus of their soul. It is he who sends dreams, and religion for the Naskapi means simply paying attention to dreams, giving them permanent form through painting and singing and attempting to understand them. Other primitive races have priests and rituals, but the rituals are based on dreams and the priests are often called to their office not by external factors but by dreams. With many primitives therefore certain dreams are discussed in public. But they are only attentive to so-called "big dreams," in which gods, spirits, cosmic events, religious and mythological motifs appear. The others, the "small dreams," merely reflect personal aspects of the dreamer and are not taken into consideration. Jung also distinguished, in a similar way, two layers of the unconscious, the "personal unconscious," which contains individual complexes, memories, repressed contents, and so on, and the "collective unconscious," in which the basic psychic structure is the same in all people and which therefore expresses itself in thoughts, feelings, emotions, and fantasies which appear in the same forms in all people. "Big dreams" come from this layer, and Jung called them "archetypal dreams." By *archetypes* he understood those innate psychic predispositions or patterns of mental behavior which are common to the human species.

In Jung's view big dreams are the primal substance in which all religions have their origin. Dreams also play an important role in the Old Testament. In the Middle Ages the church acknowledged that certain dreams can be sent by God, but admitted only those which were in accord with the teachings of the church; so dreams were censored. Jung did not accept this. He says, "Anyone who can square it with his conscience is free to decide this question as he pleases, though he may be unconsciously setting himself up as an *arbiter mundi* (judge of the world). I for my part prefer the precious gift of doubt, for the reason that it does not violate the virginity of things beyond our ken."[14] By these "things beyond our ken" Jung refers to the mysterious world of the unconscious, from which dreams emerge and whose depths we can never truly fathom.

Jung carefully wrote all of his dreams in a book especially kept for that purpose and painted illustrations to accompany them. He urged his patients and friends to do the same. He treated a dream like a crystal which one turns round and round in one's hands in order to light up all its facets. But when he understood through a dream what the unconscious wanted of him he obeyed immediately. For instance, in his younger years he and a friend once took a bicycle tour in Italy. On the trip he dreamed of an old wise man who put questions to him, and he understood from their context that he should occupy himself with certain mythological texts which at the time contained for him still unresearched problems and which, he suspected, foreshadowed his future work. Although he was only planning to stay three more days in Italy, he loaded his bicycle on the train and returned home, very much to the anger of his companion. But he obeyed immediately, so seriously did he take his dreams.

The counterbalancing, healing function of dreams probably also has an effect on people who pay no attention to them; but when one does pay attention and when one understands them, then the effect is tremendously reinforced and is therefore, in Jung's view, one of the best means of dealing with psychic problems and inner disorientations. But even more, dreams help us achieve our inner wholeness, that state which Jung has called "individuation."

When we pay attention to our dreams a self-regulating tendency in the soul comes into play which counterbalances the one-sidedness of consciousness or completes it so that a kind of wholeness and a life's optimum is achieved. The typical transitions in an individual's life which bring about his gradual maturation—as, for instance, puberty, marriage, retreat from life in old age, preparation for death—are arranged for and supported by dreams. It is interesting that the dreams of people shortly before death do not present death as an end but as an alteration of condition, for instance, through images of a long journey, of moving to another house, or of a reunion with people who have already died.

The dreams of creative individuals are especially meaningful. We know from the history of science that many great discoveries, even in chemistry and mathematics, have been inspired by dreams. The Russian chemist Dmitry Mendeleyev, for instance, who discovered the order of the elements according to their atomic weight, experimented one evening with a set of cards, as if he were playing a game of solitaire, to determine their order and did arrange such an order. That night he dreamed that his system was basically correct but that he must rotate it 180 degrees. He did this the following day and the order was then altogether correct! It is well known that poets and painters often draw their inspiration from dreams.

Robert Louis Stevenson, for instance, dreamed the basic theme
of his novel *Dr. Jekyll and Mr. Hyde*. With Jung one could even
say that he based his life work on a meticulous consideration
of his dreams. For instance, before he devoted himself to the
symbolism of alchemy, he dreamed repeatedly of discovering
a wing or an annex in his house which until then was unknown
to him. There, in a subsequent dream, he discovered a magnif-
icent library with books from the sixteenth and seventeenth
centuries. Some of the volumes contained engravings with
strange symbols. Around the same time as the dreams he
received an alchemcial book which he had ordered from a
bookseller and which contained exactly the same pictures. He
realized then how vital it was for him to study that particular
symbolism. Such an encounter between a dream motif and an
outer event with an identical meaning, in which it cannot be
proven that the one was produced causally by the other, Jung
called a "synchronistic phenomenon." If you observe your
dreams regularly, you will see that such meaningful coinci-
dences of outer and inner events do occur with relative fre-
quency. In this way one comes face to face with the as yet
unfathomed secret, the relation between the unconscious and
matter, between depth psychology and atomic physics. According to one of Jung's final hypotheses, the pathway lies
through numbers.

Jung felt that through the unconscious, that is, through his
dreams and waking fantasies, he had received a message which
concerned not only him personally but many others as well.
He understood that he should have a primal experience, then
realize it in his work. He says, "It was then that I dedicated
myself to service of the psyche. I loved it and hated it, but it
was my greatest wealth. My delivering myself over to it, as it
were, was the only way by which I could endure my existence
and live it as fully as possible."[15] This "service of the psyche"
to which Jung dedicated himself, like a knight to his Mistress
Soul, was rewarding for him; he had deeper and more impressive dreams than other people, and at the end of his life, a few
days before his death, he had a dream which he was able to
communicate: He saw a round stone above him in a high

place—the Stone of the Wise—and on it were engraved the words "And this shall be a sign to you of Wholeness and Oneness."

Notes

1. C. G. Jung, *Memories, Dreams, Reflections,* ed. Aniela Jaffé, trans. Richard and Clara Winston (New York: Random House, 1989), p. 4.
2. Ibid., p. 5.
3. Ibid., pp. 11f.
4. This sentence is missing in the Winston translation of *Memories, Dreams, Reflections,* p. 15 [—Ed.].
5. Ibid.
6. Ibid., p. 14.
7. Ibid., pp. 44f.
8. Ibid., p. 66.
9. Ibid., p. 91.
10. Cf. ibid., pp. 158ff.
11. Ibid., p. 133.
12. Ibid., p. 175.
13. Ibid., p. 176.
14. C. G. Jung, *Psychology and Alchemy, CW* 12, par. 8.
15. *Memories, Dreams, Reflections,* p. 192.

The
Dream of
Socrates

Translated by Elizabeth Welsh

In his recent book on Socrates,[1] Olaf Gigon sifted and analyzed the so-called Socratic tradition with true philological penetration. He came to the conclusion that when the question of the historical personality of Socrates is raised, we are bound to acknowledge that we know next to nothing about him.[2] What we do know is that he was an Athenian, the son of a stonemason and sculptor, Sophroniscus, that he was born circa 470 B.C. and died in prison, after having been condemned to death, in 399 B.C.—also that the accusation brought against him was that he introduced new divinities and corrupted the young—an accusation which unfortunately cannot be interpreted unequivocally. Perhaps his ugly, almost grotesque appearance, which seems to suggest a sensual nature, and the fact that he possessed a *daimonion*—whatever that may have been—should be added to the historical picture. Everything else, in the stupendous literature concerning him, is full of contradictions. In these writings he is only an image which each author and each text describes in a different way; thus, as Gigon says, he was a "pure impulse," a primordial force "which we may perhaps sense but can never name." Gigon goes on to say that most of the tradition concerning Socrates is not only "unconsciously" inaccurate, but deliberate fiction, in the sense of being an intentional deviation from the factual material.[3]

At first sight, there is actually little to add or to object to in this from our psychological point of view. Instead of speaking of a primordial force, we should formulate it rather differently and say that Socrates had evidently attracted the projection of an archetypal image, presumably the primordial image of the wise old man, and that each of his pupils, inspired and at the same time blinded by this projection, made a different picture of him.

We might be justified up to a certain point in questioning the theory of a deliberate invention. Gigon's criticism that Plato's dialogues contain unhistorical details applies only to the framework of his treatise, for instance, names, age, and so on, of the speakers. But this does not prove that Plato is unreliable insofar as the main content of the dialogues is concerned. Indeed I feel convinced that in all that touched the character of his revered master, he endeavored to be as loyal as possible. All this, however, would hardly be worth a discussion if the Platonic dialogues did not give us two of Socrates' dreams,[4] which so far philologists have not regarded as authentic historical material. There is, to be sure, an interesting attempt to interpret one of the dreams by G. D. Castelli,[5] but I intend to pursue the interpretation a good deal further than he does.

The first dream is well known; it concerns the famous passage in the *Phaedo* where Cebes asks Socrates why he has put Aesop's fables into verse and composed a hymn to Apollo. Socrates answers that he did so:

> that I might discover the meaning of certain dreams, and discharge my conscience[a]—if *this* should happen to be the music which they often ordered me to apply myself to. For they were to the following purport; often in my past life the same dream visited me, appearing at *different times* in *different forms,* yet always saying the same thing: "Socrates," it said, "make music and work."[b] And I formerly supposed that it exhorted and

[a] Fulfill his religious duty.

[b] The last sentence of the translation has been altered here to agree more closely with the Greek text.

encouraged me to continue the pursuit I was engaged in, as those who cheer on races, so that the dream encouraged me to continue the pursuit I was engaged in, namely to apply myself to music, since philosophy is the highest *mousiké* [music], and I was devoted to it.[a] But now since my trial took place, and the festival of the god retarded my death, it appeared to me that, if by chance the dream so frequently enjoined me to apply myself to popular music, I ought not to disobey it but do so. . . . Thus, then, I first of all composed a hymn to the god whose festival was present (Apollo) and put into verse those fables of Aesop. . . .[6]

According to Jung's interpretation, this should be taken as a compensating dream.[7] Socrates' attitude was too rational, and the unconscious tried in vain to warn him that he must turn his attention to the development of his feeling side. That Socrates himself did not understand the dream is clearly shown by the fact that before his death he was plagued by doubt and resorted to the inadequate, primitive expedient of carrying out the command in the dream literally. We have, however, a second dream. In the *Crito,* in which you will remember Crito offers his friend money and the means of escape to Thessaly, which Socrates refuses, ostensibly because he will not disobey the law, the following conversation occurs:[8] Crito says he has had bad news: the ship from Delos has been sighted and is expected on the following day, so that Socrates will have to die the day after tomorrow. Socrates replies that he does not believe it will arrive tomorrow.[b] He takes his evidence for this from a dream which he had only a short time before this same night, and indeed Crito had very nearly waked him at the wrong moment.

Socrates then relates his dream:

---

[a] In the sense of "anything in the domain of the muses."

[b] "Tomorrow" in our reckoning of time would mean "this evening" after 6 P.M.; for in Athens the day began at six in the evening. Hence "today" means our "today" up until 6 P.M., and "not tomorrow" means "not this evening."

Socrates: I thought I saw the fair form of a beautiful woman approaching me, clothed in bright[a] raiment, and she called to me, saying: 'O Socrates, the third day hence to cloddy[b] Phthia shalt thou come![c]

Crito: What a singular dream, Socrates.

Socrates: There can be no doubt about the meaning, Crito, I think.

Crito: Yes, the meaning is only too clear.[d]

Olaf Gigon says of this episode that it "gives the impression of a peculiar interlude without any deeper meaning."[9]

In order to be able to judge whether such a dream is a literary fiction or a genuine one, we have no a priori symptom to go by. Therefore no other choice remains but to analyze it quite naively, without any preconceived ideas, according to our methods. If we find that it yields more than we could possibly read into it, however hard we try, that is, that it produces that astounding meaning, apparently so obvious and yet so impossible to discover, which always amazes us in a genuine dream, then it must be genuine. Since this was the very impression the dream made on me when I was trying to interpret it, I should like to present it here.

It is obvious that the white, noble figure of a woman is Socrates' anima, who has come to take him away to the land beyond, or land of the dead.[e] This belongs in principle to the widespread motif according to which before the death of a man his "bush soul," or his "double" or soul-image, is likely to appear. White was also the color of the realm of the dead and of mourning in Sparta, Rome, and Messina. What surprised me was that this anima figure should appear in so white and noble a form, when we know that Socrates was married to Xanthippe and was never able to make anything approach-

---

[a] The original Greek text has "white." "Bright" is a liberty of the translator.

[b] Or "clayey," meaning fruitful; see below.

[c] *"Hemati ken tritato Phthien eribolon hikoio."*

[d] Or real: *enargēs* in the language of the ancient theory of dreams is something which will come true on the objective plane.

[e] Castelli also interprets the white woman as the "messenger of death."

ing an Eros contact with any woman. On the contrary, he continued, to the end of his life, to be the lover of Athenian youths, so that we might have expected the anima in him to have remained very undeveloped. The white figure, however, recalls Diotima, the wise woman of Elis, who, as Socrates says in the *Symposium,* revealed to him the mystery of the Platonic Eros, thus initiating him into the world of ideas.

To throw light on this problem, we must first go in search of parallel modern material. In Jung's *Seminar on Children's Dreams, 1939–40*[10] a case was discussed in which a young man's anima seemed from the outset to be of such a nature that she refused to be connected with the instinctual side, so that the tendency toward a tragic split between higher and lower would appear to have existed from the very beginning. As a five-year-old boy he dreamed that he saw a girl in the lavatory, where she was washing her hands. He was very fond of the girl, but felt very shy. A painful feeling of a separation gripped him, and he woke up. So much for the dream. Later, he fell in love with a girl who had the typical elfish quality of the anima and, in consequence of not being able to relate to her, sank into a serious state of neurotic dissociation. He could neither make up his mind to marry the girl, nor could he give her up. The lavatory—according to Jung's interpretation of the dream—is the place where a boy develops his first sexual fantasies, the place where the natural functions are exercised, and where the collective unconscious images, always connected with instinctual processes, come into play; therefore the anima is to be found there. She takes the place of the mother-image, to which the sexual fantasies cannot be applied. But the girl in the dream is washing her hands, she will have nothing to do with the dreamer's unclean sexual fantasies. This leads to the beginning of a split in him. If he wishes to avoid becoming the victim of his sublime anima, who estranges him from life, he must tear himself away from her lofty, pure, ideal image in order to reach his dark side and be able to develop his animal instincts.

This fateful predisposition to a split is often to be found in men—as Jung emphasized at the time—and frequently expresses itself later in the neglect of Eros, which constitutes the essence of the anima. Sexuality per se is rarely split off, as its presence is all too evident, but the relating function is rejected and such a man will generally endeavor to *replace it by reasoning*. In so doing, however, he disappoints a woman, for the first thing she seeks in man is Eros, the possibility of relating.

The fact that the figure of the anima in Socrates' dream has such an unworldly, pure character—coupled with the fact that his wife was deeply disappointed in him and probably tried to arouse his feeling awareness by her notorious scenes—seems to me to point to the above-mentioned problem. Socrates actually did set reason in place of the relating function and prided himself on appearing detached, free, and bound neither by emotion nor feeling. The complete lack of relatedness in his famous leave-taking of his wife in the *Phaedo* is nothing short of horrifying: she had come to the prison, bringing her little boy, and when she caught sight of his friends as they entered, she wept aloud and cried, "Socrates, your friends will now converse with you for the last time and you with them." But Socrates, looking toward Crito, said; "Crito, let someone take her home." Upon which some of Crito's attendants led her away, wailing and beating herself.[11] This according to Plato. Another anecdote is even more crude. Alcibiades has been complaining to Socrates of Xanthippe's constant scenes. Socrates replies, "I am just as used to it as to the noise of a windmill. You surely stand the constant cackle of your geese on your estate."[12] Alcibiades retorts, "But the geese provide me with eggs and their young." Socrates: "So also has Xanthippe given me children."

Whether this is historically true or not, Xanthippe has become the prototype of the excitable, wildly emotional counterpart to a philosopher. Disappointed and driven to despair by Socrates' indifference, which was admired by his followers as philosophical superiority and *apatheia*, Xanthippe reacted accordingly. Lamprocles, Socrates' eldest son, is said to have suffered considerably from his mother's behavior,[13] and his alleged death before that of his father may well have been connected with this conflict. Contrary to Plato's *Apology*, an old story[14] says that Socrates had three sons and that two of them died before their father. When during one of his philosophical discourses, someone came to inform Socrates that his son Sophronicus had died, he is said to have quietly continued, to remark later on, "Let us now go and discharge our duty to Sophronicus as the law prescribes." These stories show clearly that Socrates certainly had no firm connection with the world through his feeling function, indeed, he consciously shunned every kind of tie. Hence the white "otherworldly" color of the anima figure, who evidently did not become pure and white at the end of his life, but had never really entered the multicolored web of life at all.

The three days' respite, still accorded to Socrates in the dream, must be taken in the first place as an objective statement, that is, related to outer reality. This is also the conclusion Socrates himself drew from the dream. The symbolical aspect, however, cannot be completely overlooked; Socrates might have had the dream the night before or the night after—why then precisely *three* days? Besides the countless other aspects attached to the meaning of the number three, it is particularly associated with the gods connected with fate, as for example the three Norns, the old German goddesses of fate; the three Moirae of the Greeks; and the Parcae of the Romans (whom we call the three Fates) and so forth; and further with the symbolism of time, with its three phases of past, present, and future. In fairy tales the hero and heroine usually go through three similar stages, encountering three witches' houses, three hermits, three helpers such as Sun, Moon, and Wind, before reaching the coveted goal. Moreover, "three" is mostly connected with a dynamic process or sequence of events which takes place in time.[15] Hence, on account of this dynamic element, which relates it to the instinctual realm, the "three is often associated with the chthonic gods, Hecate, Cerberus, and so on, who represent the forces of instinct. The motif of the three stages in fairy tales is also to be understood in the sense of: 1—2—3 and then comes the lysis: 4! There are actually thus four, but the fourth does not belong to a dynamic course of events; it is the goal itself, stabilization outside time. In the dream under consideration here we have the same situation: three days and then comes the arrival in Phthia, in the land of the dead, where time no longer exists. The three days tell us that now an inevitable fate is being fulfilled, *that a psychological course is beginning, which consciousness is incapable of altering in any way.*

Had Socrates still considered the possibility of escape, the dream shows by this motif of the "three" that for inner reasons he can no longer do so.

After interpreting the boy's dream quoted above, as showing a form of the anima problem, Jung goes on to say that in such a case a young man should try to escape from the anima and fight his way down into the world in order to develop by means of his instinctive side. He must descend into reality through the dark vale of his instincts, for the way to the discovery of woman leads from below upward, and not from above downward. This is the "gruesome, muddy, hollow way leading to Aphrodite's pleasant grove," the thought of which caused even a Parmenides to shudder.[16] To take this path means a painful separation from the fascination of the bright anima figure.

If courage to tear oneself free is lacking, there is the danger of becoming possessed by the soul-image. A man then becomes identical with his anima and frequently succumbs to homosexuality.[17] To what extent the anima in Socrates' case was "She Who Must Be Obeyed," the *Crito* dialogue[18] shows in a very impressive way: seen from a rational point of view, from outside, it was easy for Socrates to escape from prison, but he remained faithful to his dream. He describes this faithfulness as obedience to the laws of Athens, but it is personified in a feminine form that he makes the *polis* (town) plead with him: "We have brought you into the world . . . nurtured and educated you . . ." How then, questions Socrates, could he do violence to his *patris* (f., native town) or *polis* (f., state)? The "polis" is clearly to be understood here as a mother figure, as *metr*opolis. And this finally leads us to the actual main point: this form of the anima is simply a facet of the *mother image,* it is a *far too lofty ideal of the feminine principle,* *which is experienced by a son who clings to his mother with an exaggerated feeling of reverence. To be unable to break away from this figure and reach the world is a characteristic of the mother complex.*[19] The individual law of development, which would demand temporary unfaithfulness and separation from the mother, is thus bypassed.[20] Not to escape from this anima, but to fall in love with her, means, as Jung says, being enticed away from life. This anima-possession seems often to be supported by a simultaneous father complex, when circumstances make it difficult for the son to grow up under a father who overshadows him. In this connection we have a singular tale concerning Socrates which Plutarch has preserved. His father, the stonemason and sculptor Sophroniscus, is said to have been directed by the gods to allow the child to do just what came into his head, and simply to pray for him to Zeus Agoraios and the Muses; for Socrates had been given a guide for life, who was better than a thousand teachers and educators—this referred to the *daimonion.*[21] But surely Sophroniscus would never have received such advice from the gods had he not shown a tendency to restrain the child and bring it up much too severely.

We know practically nothing of Socrates' mother; it is striking that he never alludes to her in the Platonic dialogues, except once, but then most significantly, at the end of the *Theaetetus,* when he describes his art of educating youth as *maieutic*—as the midwife's skill. In this passage he says that he seeks young men with richly endowed and "pregnant" minds and by his questionings and testings he clears away the hindrances that stand in the way of bringing to birth these germs of thought.[22] He ends the dialogue as follows: "Both I and my mother received this midwife function from God—she with regard to women, I, on the other hand, concerning young men who are efficient and good . . ." Thus Socrates is identified with his mother, it is *her* profession which he practices in the psychological and intellectual realm. He is so completely enveloped by the mother-anima figure, that it is only through her that he is able to influence the world and his fellow men. *The white woman of his dream and Diotima are certainly also images of the mother. In this case, however, the mother signifies the world beyond, paradise, the memory of the archetypal images, from which he who is born into the world should tear himself free.*[23] It is dangerous, Jung says, for a man to remain caught in this lost world, because he then avoids touching the earth, and so will never be born. Such people give the impression of a curiously arrested development. They cannot touch the world and take it, so to speak, in their fingers because it is dirty. A man who is under the spell of the anima to such an extent becomes incompetent, because his development has been arrested. In this connection we should remember that Socrates was accused of *argia*, of idleness and of leading youth astray into idleness. Here I must return to a point in the first-mentioned dream. The command in the dream in Greek is as follows: "O Sokrates, mousikén póiei kái ergázon," which is usually interpreted as "Make music and work at it." But I think it might rather mean: "Make music and work"—namely, that the dream orders him to do two things, to make music, in other words to develop his feeling function, *and* to work, in order that he might reach and actually enter the reality of the earth, in the sense mentioned above, instead of spending all his time philosophizing in the *agora*, the marketplace. True, only the artisans, from whose class Socrates sprang, worked in Athens, not the rich; but the rich had political duties. Socrates, however, was kept out of politics by his *daimonion*, and so did not work at all; this his opponents considered a scandal.[24]

The identity with the mother, and the idea that Socrates practiced her profession, coincide in a significant way with the fact that, according to tradition, Socrates was born at the so-called Thargelia.[a] The month called Thargelion, the eleventh in the Athenian year, lasted from about 24 April to 24 May.[25] On 6 and 7 Thargelion, the festival of the Thargelia was celebrated, a harvest festival at which the first fruits of the field were offered to the gods. The sixth day of the month, Socrates' birthday, was held to be the birthday of Artemis Eleithya, the helper in childbirth, therefore the midwife-goddess! Her

[a] Plural of *Thargelion*.

priestesses wore white garments. This Artemis is not the slender huntress known to us in Hellenistic art, but an imposing mother goddess, often portrayed with many breasts.[26] The seventh day of Thargelion was Apollo's birthday and was alleged to be Plato's also. In earlier times, on the sixth day of Thargelion, a peculiar custom took place: two particularly ugly and bodily misshapen creatures, a man and a woman, were selected, decked—he with dark-colored figs and she with white figs—and led outside the town, where they were solemnly cursed, every kind of disease and evil being wished on to them. In still earlier days they were burned on the spot. It was therefore a purification ritual, corresponding to that of the Jewish scapegoat. These victims were called *pharmakoi,* from *pharmakon* ("remedy"), because they healed the town (cleansed it from sin). Toward the end of the fifth century, the custom of human sacrifice had ceased to exist in Greece and the *pharmakoi* were only cursed, but not killed. It is really singular to recall that Socrates was renowned for his ugliness, and that historians, though quite oblivious of the traditional parallel, have often stressed the point that the case against Socrates was instigated with the object of finding a scapegoat, in order to provide the people of Athens, who were in an excited and dissatisfied mood following the unhappy outcome of the Peloponnesian War, with a sensation, as a diversion—a sort of lightning conductor. The Athenian calendar of feast days, like astrological symbolism, is, so to speak, a projection of archetypal images into the flow of time, and, seen in this symbolically qualified space of time, Socrates was undoubtedly born a *pharmakos*. According to the legend, the prototype of these people who were sacrificed was a man called Pharmakos, an enemy of Achilles,[a] who was stoned by the latter for desecrating a temple.

This brings us to the second part of the sentence in the dream concerning "cloddy Phthia." The epithet *eribōlos* applied to Phthia means "very cloddy," and in those southern regions, where the soil is mostly light and sandy instead of

---

[a] For the meaning of Achilles in relation to Socrates, see below.

clayey, it has the same significance as "fruitful." The earthy, even claylike aspect of the Beyond and the Land of the Dead is emphatically stressed, presumably as a compensation for Socrates' life, which was so far removed from the earth.

In this connection we should ask what actually was Socrates' attitude to the world of impelling urges and instincts. His attitude appears to have been remarkably superior and detached. His estrangement from nature is evident in the introductory dialogue in the *Phaedrus,* where he admits to his companion, who has led him to a pleasant seat under a plane tree, that he has practically never left the city, for "trees and fields cannot teach me anything, but men in the city can."[27] And what is his connection with animals? You probably know the anecdote according to which the *daimonion* warned him, when he was walking through Athens in deep conversation with a friend, to take a side street, and he had no sooner done so than a large herd of pigs came rushing down the street, trampling down and bespattering all the passersby, including his friends, who had not suddenly turned off as he had.[28] A remarkable old report also explained that the accusation brought against Socrates that he sought to introduce new divinities[29] meant that he recommended the worship of dogs and birds.[30] His favorite oath, "pros kyna" ("by the dog"), was interpreted in this sense. Besides there is no doubt that his animal nature in general was projected on Xanthippe whom in the anecdotes he always compares to a horse that is difficult to ride,[31] a goose, and so on. The reports dealing with this whole question appear to me to be too obscure to warrant any definite conclusions, but at least it seems probable that in the case of Socrates the animal nature plays an ambivalent role: spurned and at the same time "numinous." This is surely connected with his estrangement from nature and reality, which is compensated in the dream by the motif of "cloddy Phthia." It stresses, as it were, "for dust thou art, and unto dust shalt thou return." Socrates did not live the Fall, nor did he as a result of it "in the sweat of his brow eat bread," until he returned "unto the earth." This is why this return to earth only in death is emphasized. The terrifying clayey hollow path, mentioned above, which leads to Aphrodite (as Parmenides says), is also the way of death which leads to Persephone.

Phthia is actually a district in Thessaly, and the latter, lying in the center of Greece, was renowned and notorious throughout the whole of antiquity as the land of the great witches, the center of sorcery—we need only think, for instance, of Apuleius's novel *The Golden Ass.* This is the unconscious, the land of the dangerous, spellbinding image of the mother, the mother-witch, to which the white woman will lead him back. The name might possibly point to another connection where the interpretation is concerned: *Phthino* means "fading away"— the aoristic root is *phthi*—and this coupled with Socrates' own description of the land as land of the dead might well be taken into consideration.

This much can be inferred from the sentence in the dream itself, but it means a great deal more: for it is an authentic sentence in the *Iliad,* and when we insert Homer's context, a far more extensive background appears. This sentence is from the ninth book, in which delegates from the Greeks come to beg Achilles, who is raging in his tent, to reenter the battle. Achilles, as you know, is in a fury because Agamemnon has unlawfully taken away his beautiful Trojan slave, Briseis, to replace his own slave, Chryseis, whom he had to restore to her father at Apollo's command.

The mission fails and Achilles even threatens to set sail for his homeland, Phthia:[32]

Then shall you see our parting vessels crown'd
And hear with oars the Hellespont resound.
The third day hence shall Phthia[a] *greet our sails,*
If mighty Neptune send propitious gales:
Phthia to her Achilles shall restore
The wealth he left for this deserted shore.
Thither the spoils of this long war shall pass,
The ruddy gold, the steel, the shining brass.

---

[a] Voss's German translation, quoted by the author, has "cloddy Phthia," and some English translations have "fruitful Phthia." (—TRANS.)

My beauteous captives thither I'll convey,
And all that rests of my unravish'd prey.

And further down:

If heaven restore me to my realms with life,
The reverend Peleus[a] shall elect my wife;
Thessalian nymphs there are of form divine,
And kings that sue to mix their blood with mine.
Bless'd in kind love, my years shall glide away,
Content with just hereditary sway;

However, as you will remember, this does not happen. Patro-
cles fights for the Greeks in Achilles' armor and falls. Achilles
is again drawn into the battle to avenge him and is slain by an
arrow from the bow of Paris, which Apollo guides.

The verse quoted in Socrates' dream therefore alludes to this
whole passage in the text: Socrates himself is tired of fighting
like Achilles, he is disappointed and injured and would gladly
return to the land of his home, where he could find his bride.
Achilles is a figure in Socrates himself:[b] he is that part of him
which, as a *minythadiós* is one destined to die young, has not
been able to grow up and has been cheated of his union with
the feminine principle for which he yearned. He is also the
man of deeds, whom Socrates, the thinker and talker, never
allowed to develop in himself, the *hero in him who wanted to live
life at all costs and was not able to.* Socrates undoubtedly projected
this "inner Achilles" on all those young friends whom he was
anxious to make *agathoi* (efficient) and *esthloi* (noble), and in
whom through projection he tried to develop "outside" that
which in himself had still remained young and disappointed in
life.[c] Agamemnon can also be interpreted as a figure in Socra-

---

[a] Father of Achilles.

[b] Compare also Castelli, *Posdomani a Ftia* (Verona, 1951), p. 17ff. He quite
independently comes to the conclusion that Achilles is an inner figure in
Socrates.

[c] It might be objected here that Socrates was very heroic in the Delian war
episode, so that he did live the "man of action," but in my opinion this "inner
Achilles" only broke through from time to time, but was not integrated in
Socrates' life.

tes himself: he is the king and therefore the much too rational
ruling spirit in Socrates, who robs Achilles of his beloved.
(You will remember that the Pharmakos was an enemy of
Achilles.)ᵃ The *puer aeternus* in Socrates was never able to
develop further, through union with the feminine principle,
into a "divine pair."

Achilles himself, who, as Socrates would have known, was
worshiped ritually as a hero and even as a god in many parts
of Greece, particularly in Thessaly, is a semidivine, short-lived
mother's son. His sister is Philomela. He was also believed to
be *apó dryós é pétras,* which means born "from an oak or a
stone" like Mithras. His mother, Thetis, is a sea goddess, a
Nereid, who was worshiped in many places as a serpent;
according to another version she is the daughter of the centaur
Chiron. Having given her mortal husband, Peleus, a son,
Achilles, she wanted to make him immortal and hardened him
every night in the fire or in hot water, but the heel by which
she held him remained vulnerable and it was there that he was
mortally wounded. According to another version, she was
trying to kill him by her magic tricks, but when Peleus
surprised her in the act, she gave them up. Thus although the
positive aspect of the mother archetype undoubtedly comes to
the fore as the white woman in Socrates' dream, the dark,
deadly aspect is also hinted at, just as the white woman leads
Socrates into the witches' country.

Jung once said that the man who is bound to his mother is
in constant danger of running back to her whenever he meets
with the disappointments which life provides, in order to
receive from her what he was incapable of winning by his own
effort. This will remind you of the episode in the first book of
the *Iliad,* where Achilles complains to Thetis of the loss of
Briseis, of whom he has been robbed:³³

She [Briseis], in soft sorrows and in pensive thought,
Pass'd silent, as the heralds held her hand,

ᵃ Achilles is the "most beautiful of all the Greeks," Socrates the ugly, "cabir-
like" man, and yet Achilles is also one of the Kabeiroi (cabiri).

And oft looked back, slow-moving o'er the strand.
Not so his loss the fierce Achilles bore;
But sad, retiring to the sounding shore,
O'er the wild margin of the deep he hung,
That kindred deep from whence his mother sprung:
There bathed in tears of anger and disdain,
Thus loud lamented to the stormy main:
"O parent goddess! since in early bloom
Thy son must fall, by too severe a doom;
Sure to so short a race of glory born,
Great Jove in justice should this span adorn.
Honour and fame at least the thunderer owed;
And ill he pays the promise of a god,
If yon proud monarch thus thy son defies,
Obscures my glories, and resumes my prize."
Far from the deep recesses of the main,
Where aged Ocean holds her watery reign,
The goddess-mother heard. The waves divide;
And like a mist she rose above the tide;
Beheld him mourning on the naked shores,
And thus the sorrows of his soul explores.
"Why grieves my son?[a] Thy anguish let me share;
Reveal the cause, and trust a parent's care!"
He deeply sighing said: "To tell my woe
Is but to mention what too well you know."

And then, complaining bitterly, he tells his sorrows to his
"silver-footed" mother, and begs her to intercede for him with
Zeus, that he may cause the Trojans to advance:

"But, goddess! Thou thy suppliant son attend.
To high Olympus' shining court ascend,
Urge all the ties to former service owed,
And sue for vengeance to the thundering god."[34]

. . . .

"Unhappy son (fair Thetis thus replies,
While tears celestial trickle from her eyes)
Why have I borne thee with a mother's throes,
To Fates adverse, and nursed for future woes?

[a] The Greek work is *pepon* (baby)!

So short a space the light of heaven to view!
So short a space! And filled with sorrow too!
O might a parent's careful wish prevail,
Far, far from Ilion should thy vessels sail,
And thou, from camps remote, the danger shun
Which now, alas! too nearly threats my son.
Yet (what I can) to move thy suit I'll go
To great Olympus crown'd with fleecy snow.
Meantime, secure within thy ships, from far
Behold the field, nor mingle in the war."[35]

It should be noted here that Thetis no longer lives with her mortal husband, Peleus, but in the sea with the sea-god, her grey father.[a]

Our justification, however, for taking Achilles as an inner figure in Socrates does not rest only on the verse in the dream. In the *Apology*,[36] Plato makes Socrates reason as follows:

Some will say: And are you not ashamed, Socrates, of a course of life which is likely to bring you to an untimely end? To him I may fairly answer: There you are mistaken: a man who is good for anything ought not to calculate the chance of living or dying; he ought only to consider whether in doing anything he is doing right or wrong—acting the part of a good man or of a bad. Whereas, upon your view, the heroes who fell at Troy were not good for much, *and the son of Thetis above all, who altogether despised danger in comparison with disgrace* and when he was so eager to slay Hector, his goddess mother said to him . . . that if he avenged his companion Patroclus and slew Hector, he would die himself. "Fate," she said in these or the like words, "waits for you next after Hector." He, receiving this warning, utterly despised danger and death, and instead of fearing them, feared rather to live in dishonor[b] and not avenge his friend. "Let me die forthwith," he replies, "and be avenged of my enemy, rather than abide here by the beaked ships, a laughing-stock and a burden of the earth."

Thus, when Socrates deliberately brings death upon himself, he identifies with Achilles, who, instead of returning to Phthia,

---

[a] A whole incestuous chain of connections.

[b] Literally as a *kakos* (an inferior man, a menial or serf).

dies avenging Patroclus. By his refusal, in the very last hours of his life, to obey the mother-complex, he allows the "man of deeds" to break through just as Achilles plunged into the battle; he breaks through the shell of the "maternal" image enveloping him and, as if were, dying reaches reality. This is no doubt why, as his last words in the *Phaedo* so beautifully imply, he experienced death as "recovery from the long disease of life." After death, however, as the dream forecasts, his mother will fetch him home to the prenatal fields, where the eternal youth in him will be able to marry; in other words attain complete fulfillment. Legend[37] has it that Achilles, after his death, was united with the beautiful Helen on the island of Leuke.[a] The moon-island of Leuke is the home of white birds.[38] It seems as if the Self had lost patience with Socrates and all hope of his ever being able to reach his goal in this life—the *daimonion* namely refused to allow him to prepare a defense in the *agora*.[39] Seen in the light of all these connections, it is no longer absurd, but indeed remarkably and profoundly significant, that the Middle Ages should have looked upon Socrates as a forerunner or prefiguration of Christ, for Saint Augustine also interpreted death on the cross as marriage with the mother.

This leads us to the discussion of a further problem, namely, what was that mysterious *daimonion* of Socrates'? In the first place, we hear from Xenophon that it was a *semainein,* an "indication";[40] others—and Plato among them—described it as a *phonē* (voice); it was also called a divine sign (*semeion*), and occasionally a sound (*echo*).[41] Plutarch cites the theory of a certain Therpsion, according to which it was a "sneeze," either one's own or another's, from which Socrates was evidently able to read a mantic sign. As a mantic technique of sneezing existed at that time,[42] this might well be a misinterpretation. Actually, the *daimonion* plays an important role in Socrates' relations with his friends. In the pseudo-Platonic treatise called the *Great Alcibiades* we read that the *daimonion* allowed the

---

[a] This is probably behind the German youths' romantic lovesick "yearning for death."

connection with Alcibiades only after the latter had sacrificed his earlier aims and friends and was ready for higher aims and relationships. When a pupil of Socrates' who had left the latter for a time wanted to resume the connection again, the *daimonion* forbade it. Another pupil, Aristeides, made great strides in philosophy while he was in contact with Socrates, and then left the circle to take part in a campaign. When he came back he had lost all capacity for sustaining an argument. Socrates asked him the reason for this regression, to which he replied that he never really learned anything from Socrates, but that it was rather owing to the latter's presence in the same house, or room, that he became wise. He had made the greatest strides whenever he sat close to Socrates and touched him.[43] Frequently the *daimonion* gives a warning through Socrates when a friend in the circle is planning something, and in general its effect is to restrain and warn, likewise where Socrates himself is concerned; but it is never active or commanding. In the *Politeia,* Socrates tells Theages that by nature he (Theages) is made for politics, but that he is too sickly. He himself (Socrates) is in a similar situation with regard to the *daimonion,* but one cannot speak about it, for it is a queer thing.[44]

In the light of our present-day psychological knowledge, we should obviously be inclined to identify Socrates' *daimonion* with a part of his unconscious personality, or even with the Self—and I am of the opinion that in principle this is the right interpretation. Nevertheless, in view of the completely different circumstances at that time, we are bound to make certain distinctions. In the first place, one cannot help being struck by the fact that the *daimonion* ruled supreme over all of Socrates' human relations. This confirms our earlier discovery that Eros is missing in Socrates' conscious life; in other words, his feeling function has remained completely in the unconscious and bound to the contents of the unconscious. His only real love was for his mother, the sphere of the archetypal images. This is why his friends often found him so unrelated. In Xenophon's *Symposium,* Antisthenes reproaches him as follows:[45] "You are ever the same, sometimes you make use of the 'daimonion' as an excuse when you do not wish to talk to me and at other times you are taken up with other people." Thus, in Socrates the Self seems to be contaminated with the function of relationship, the anima, and appears also in a certain paradoxical double aspect, both light and dark. It could be compared to the alchemistic Mercurius, who was both trickster and savior at the same time. Speaking of the latter, Jung says:

> He is physical and spiritual . . . he is the devil . . . an evasive trickster and the Divinity, as the latter is portrayed in maternal nature. He is the reflected image of a mystical experience of the artifex, which coincides with the *opus alchymicum*. As this experience, he represents on the one hand the Self and on the other the process of individuation; and, owing to the boundless character of his vocation, the collective unconscious as well.[46]

As Socrates never surrendered himself to the *pyr aeizóon* (eternal, living fire) of passionate instincts and never endeavored to come to terms with the *daimonion,* he remained untransformed, and the Self remained contaminated with the shadow and the anima, but as a result, it exercised a powerful *collective* influence. This probably also explains the fact that the *daimonion* only restrains and warns him, but never gives him positive advice: it always tries to force him to introvert, to turn his attention inward and thus once and for all to act as a midwife to the unborn contents in *himself.* According to the law of compensation, we should assume that Socrates' tendency was to be far too much concerned with outer things and that this explains the reason why the *daimonion* appeared as a restraining factor. From the psychological point of view, however, we are also justified in connecting the *daimonion* with the two dreams—which philologists have so far never ventured to do—for in our eyes both manifestations are part of the same unconscious personality. Then, however, it is no longer true to say that the *daimonion* appeared only as a restricting factor, for the dream urging Socrates to "make music and work" gave him, as it were, a positive indication. The statement that the figure in the dream *recurred again and again in a different form*— presumably sometimes as a god, sometimes in the shape of an animal, a man or a woman—is very significant. Since there was no attempt to come to terms with the contents of the unconscious, they were bound to remain contaminated.

As to the preponderance of the inhibiting aspect, it should be remembered that Socrates identified with the mother, that is, his attitude toward his young friends was a feminine, receptive one. His maternal behavior where his young friends were concerned appears clearly in a dream of his which is related in Apuleius's treatise *De Platone:*[47] Socrates dreamed that a young swan flew up from the altar of Eros in the Academy, alighted on his lap and then, singing most beautifully, soared up to heaven. When a few days later, Socrates made the acquaintance of the young Plato for the first time, he is supposed to have said, "So that was the swan of Eros in the Academy!" These mythological associations with the bird of Apollo have already been amplified in K. Kerényi's book *Apollon.*[48] Plato was presumably born on Apollo's birthday, on 7 Thargelion, and in the *Phaedo,* Socrates compares the soul's joy before death with the swan's song. I prefer not to go more deeply into *this* dream, as I do not feel as sure as I do regarding the Phthia-dream that it is not a subsequent invention. However this may be, in it he significantly plays the part of a mother: he takes the young swan on his lap. The dream may be genuine after all, when one recalls Eckermann's dream as a boy that he caught a beautiful bird, which doubtless points to his later friendship with Goethe.

The role of spiritual mother which Socrates plays appears also in Plato's dialogues: he is always the one who tests the statements of others, who by his practice of cross-examining shows their naivete, their superficiality, and their lack of logic, but is never the one to display his own knowledge. This passivity of mind—the lack of determination to risk himself in a creative act—makes it impossible for the unconscious to unfold its contents, because for this it needs a strong, active ego to serve as a vessel.

Here we should inquire what kind of collective images were trying to break through at that time and in what form? The Olympic gods had become ineffectual, the rural population clung as ever to its local cults, while the educated people were seized by a kind of unsatisfied seeking, which is typical of such times, when the religious contents are undergoing transformation. Then the new symbols of the unconscious broke through in two forms: (1) in the speculations of natural science, in the center of which stood the symbol of the "round thing," the *sphairos,* the idea of the circulation of energy, the image of a round cosmos, or of the whirling *nous;*[a] and (2) in the new esoteric myths of the mystery movements, colored by philosophy and theology, as in the Orphic and Dionysian mysteries. What presumably prevented Socrates from immersing himself in the latter was his fear of the inferno of instinctive urges and wild emotions, his Apollonian spirit, as Kerényi calls it. What repelled him in the speculative theories formulated in natural science was—as he says in his criticism of Anaxagoras—the fact that these theories contained too little explanation founded on fact. Both these realms of unconscious symbol-forming, from which Socrates turned away, broke through again in Plato's creative mind and were able to unfold. What Socrates aimed at with this attitude was doubtless a defensive strengthening of the *ratio,* the ego-consciousness of man. As one who was enveloped by the mother, he was bound to adopt this *defensive* attitude.

The fact that the whole abundance of the collective images stood, so to speak, behind this *daimonion* is proved, at least insofar as these images were often projected onto the *daimonion* by others. Thus Plutarch relates[49] that a certain Boeotian, Timarchus, determined to investigate Socrates' *daimonion* and descended into the cave of Trophonius for the purpose. Enveloped in darkness, he receives a blow on the head, through which his soul leaves his body, spreads itself out and, suddenly looking up, he can no longer see the earth, but perceives fire-bright islands of changing colors, circular in shape, which, while rotating, give forth sweet music. In the middle lies a sea which whirls the islands round in a circle. Streams of fire flow into the sea through two inlets and lash it into fury. In the center there is a deep circular hole, precipitous and frightful,

[a] Mind, cosmic mind, cosmic intelligence.

filled with darkness and flowing over with commotion. Issuing from it can be heard the howls and groans of animals, wailing children, and the cries of pain of men and women. A voice coming from the guardian of the underworld explains to him that the island sphere above belongs to other gods, the lower one is divided into four parts: that of life, of movement, of creation, and of destruction. One and two are connected by the invisible, two and three by the *nous* in the realm of the sun, three and four by the nature of the moon. The three Fates (Moirae) rule over these three connecting spheres. Each island has a god, only the moon flees from the Styx and is overtaken by it every one hundred and seventy-seventh second's space of time, when it is robbed of certain souls. On the other hand, the moon saves the pure souls from further generation. The *nous,* which enters the soul from outside, is the part that preserves men from sinking down into the body and its passions. People think of the *nous* as a reflection in themselves, meaning also that they are in the mirror and see out of it, but it is truer to call this the *daimonion.* After further elucidations, the voice says at last, "This, dear youth, you will get to know more definitely in three months' time—now depart." He came to himself with an aching head and died three months later— having requested to be buried next to Socrates' son Lamprocles, a request which was granted him.

This tale will show you better than anything else how completely the mysterious *daimonion* attracted the projection of the whole collective unconscious—and an uncanny breath of death and destruction hovered round it. I am also of the opinion that its effect was not without danger. Under its influence, the young writer Plato burned his creative work and did not write again until long after Socrates' death. However, the creative impulse in him was incapable of being killed by such a conscious intervention; it broke through anew, after a time, in a deeper and clearer form. Nevertheless, the daemonic power of this spirit in Socrates is undeniable.[a]

---

[a] Cf. also the "cramp-fish" anecdote in the *Meno,* where Meno twits Socrates with using "incantations to bewitch" him and likens him to the "cramp-fish, for that too never fails to give a numbness to every person who either touches or approaches it" (trans. Hayer Sydenham, in *Five Dialogues of Plato,* p. 88).

Another interesting theory is developed by Apuleius in his *Liber de deo Socratis*,[50] on a Neoplatonic basis. It refers to the original passage in the *Symposium,* where Socrates is repeating a discourse concerning love which he formerly heard from the prophetess Diotima, who taught him the science of things relating to love:[51]

Socrates: What then is that [Love]?

Diotima: A great daemon, Socrates; and everything daemonical holds an intermediate place between what is divine and what is mortal.

Socrates: What is his power and nature?

Diotima: He interprets and makes a communication between divine and human things, conveying the prayers and sacrifices of men to the Gods and communicating the commands and directions concerning the mode of worship most pleasing to them, from Gods to men. He fills that intermediate space between these two classes of beings, so as to bind together, by his own power, the whole universe of things. Through him subsist all divination, and the science of sacred things as it relates to sacrifices, and expiations, and disenchantments, and prophecy and magic. . . . These daemons are, indeed, many and various and one of them is Love!

According to Apuleius also the gods are eternal beings who can neither be reached or touched by human emotions, nor have they any direct connection with human beings. But in the between-realm of the air there are air-beings, whom the Greek call *daemones,* who carry hither and thither prayers, offerings or divine intimations (they are *"vectores precum interpretes salutigeri"*). It is they who bring about the miraculous effects of magicians and all mantic happenings in dreams, haruspicy, augury from the flight of birds, and so forth. They are like *animalia* (creatures) that live in the air and have a "subtle body" (*concretio multo subtilior,* namely, nubibus)[52] like clouds. The air is a *"media natura,"* and correspondingly the function of these, its *animalia,* is a *mediatory* function. They share with the upper gods eternal life, with the lower mortals earthly passions; they can be favorably influenced or provoked to anger. Therefore, "according to their nature the daemons are animalia, according to the spirit *rationabilia* (reasonable beings), according to their character, capable of emotions, according to their body, airy and according to time, eternal." Certain people are endowed with such daemons as individual guardian spirits, they are *eudaimones,* they have a good guardian spirit and are happy. This is the Latin idea of the *genius,* which unites body and soul; in earlier Latin they were called *lemures.* If propitiated with due rites, they become, after death, the *lar familiaris,* if not they appear as a ghost or specter. (Both are identical with the Roman *manes.*) In later times certain of these *lares* were universally worshiped in cults, for instance Mopsus in Africa, Osiris in Egypt, Amphiaraus in Boeotia. Socrates had such a good guardian spirit with him, as *"privus custos . . . domesticus speculator, proprius curator, intimus cognitor, adsiduus observator, individuus arbiter* (!) *inseparabilis testis, malorum improbator, bonorum probator . . . in rebus incertis prospector, dubiis monitor, periculosis tutator, egenis opitulator."*[a] He expresses himself in dreams, signs, or, in an emergency, as a concrete interference of fate.

So far for Apuleius, whose interpretation strikes me as particularly interesting, inasmuch as it shows what kind of projection the "numinous" background of Socrates' personality has attracted to itself. Apart from this, however, we should think over the following problem: what are these daemons of the between-world from a psychological point of view?

The gods obviously represent the archetypes, in their "psychoid" absolute essence, remote from consciousness; the daemons, on the other hand, who, as eternal beings, must likewise embody archetypal contents, represent them in an aspect which is nearer consciousness and particularly in the aspect of

[a] Chapter 16. ". . . our guardian; our watcher at home, our own proper regulator, a searcher into our inmost fibres, our constant observer, our inseparable witness, a reprover of our evil actions, an approver of our good ones . . . our forewarner in uncertainty, our monitor in matters of doubt, our defender in danger, and our assistant in need" ("The God of Socrates," in *The Works of Apuleius* [London: G. Bell and Sons, 1911]).

an instinctual, dynamic factor which releases emotions. They possess a "subtle body"; taken literally, therefore, they are relatively more fully incarnated. In *Der Geist der Psychologie*,[53] Jung says that the archetype in itself is presumably beyond conscious experience, that is, transcendent, and should therefore be defined as psychoid. In contrast to this are the archetypal ideas which the unconscious conveys to us. The archetype belongs to a realm which in this sense[54] therefore cannot ultimately be called psychic, although it manifests itself psychically. In my opinion the Olympic gods in Apuleius's theory represent this aspect of the archetype; the daemons, on the other hand, its *psychic* manifestations in the unconscious. Thus, in these interpretations of late antiquity (much more than two thousand years have elapsed since Socrates' death), we find attempts to interpret the *daimonion* which recall the Christian idea of incarnation. Christ was defined as "true God" and "true man" (*vere deus, vere homo*), but in Docetism or in the legends related in Gnostic texts, the fusion of both aspects into one is still distinctly uncertain. However, the Greek theory of the *daimonion* is, as it were, a first attempt at a formulation which points in the same direction.

The astonishing fact in Socrates' life is that, unlike Pythagoras or Empedocles, he did not assume the role of an immortal daemon or god. This brings us to the positive aspect of his attitude of restraint over against the creative urge of the unconscious images: this awe or reserve prevented a harmful identification with these images and an inflation such as overcame so many of his forerunners. I believe this to be the meaning of the famous Socratic irony. It acts as a constant defensive mechanism in its owner and in others against the danger of inflation. His *eironeia* (irony) often had on others the effect of *alazoneia* (provocative boastfulness). Seen in this connection, Socrates strove for an increase of consciousness, which aimed at giving the ego a stronger and more definite boundary over against the contents of the unconscious. His lack of interest in the speculations of natural science and mythology and his exclusive interest in the human being presumably come from the same need. Thus, in spite of his problem described above,

Socrates had somehow more individuality than a Pythagoras or an Empedocles and thus his fate can be considered as an example of a certain stage in the process of individuation. What Plato makes Alcibiades say of Socrates in the *Symposium* is, in this sense, most apt. He compares him to one of the insignificant statues of Silenus on the roadside: "And as carved Sileni are made to encase (golden) images of gods, so this Silenus-mask[a] entreasures things divine." This means that he is attracting archetypal contents and so drawing them into the realm of the human psyche. Socrates is described as the shrine, or vessel (again in the feminine role). In order to keep him in this role, the *daimonion* prevented him from becoming active in political life; beyond this, however, the dream endeavored to make him give these images of the gods a creative reality in the psychic realm, and thereby a way was prepared for a step forward in consciousness which, however, was only to be more fully realized later: dimly in alchemy and with increasing clearness in modern psychology. At that time, the challenge of the unconscious or of the Self—Socrates would have said *ho theós*—was certainly still too great. The time was not yet ripe for such a far-reaching withdrawal of projections from the realm of the gods, and the marriage of Achilles in Phthia, the motif of the marriage of King and Queen, which was to become so significant in alchemy, remains a postmortal expectation here. Death therefore holds a promise and is described at the same time as the marriage of the divine pair and the return to the native soil and the mother. Hence, to my mind, in the realm of Greek culture it is in Socrates that the problem of individuation emerged for the first time from the stage in which its images were completely projected into the mythological world or into nature and was brought appreciably nearer individual man—heralded by the symptom of that deep suffering and of the painful split which was to characterize the Christian era.

The dream in *Crito*, however, with its allusion to the ancient hero-image Achilles and his mother, reveals, as it were, the

[a] I.e., Socrates.

hidden individual constellation of the problem, which makes the personality of Socrates so significant and at the same time so difficult to understand. Therefore it seems to me that we may nevertheless be justified in attributing even profound historical significance to this "peculiar interlude," as Gigon calls it.

Notes

1. Olaf Gigon, *Sokrates: Sein Bild in Dichtung und Geschichte* (Bern: A. Francke, 1947).
2. Ibid., p. 16.
3. Ibid., p. 59ff.
4. There is also a further dream in Apuleius, *De Platone*, Lib. I, 1.
5. G. D. Castelli, *Posdomani a Ftia* (Verona, 1951). What Castelli emphasizes is the anima problem.
6. Plato, *Phaedo*, Henry Cary, in *Five Dialogues of Plato* (London: J. M. Dent, 1917) p. 137.
7. C. G. Jung, *English Seminar on the Interpretation of Visions* (Zurich: multigraphed typescript, 1930), vol. 1, p. 13ff.
8. Plato, *Crito* 44. Cf. *The Works of Plato*, trans. Henry Cary (London: Henry G. Bohn, 1848), vol. 1, p. 32.
9. Gigon, *Sokrates*, pp. 82–83.
10. C. G. Jung, *Psychologische Interpretation von Kinderträumen* (Zurich: multigraphed typescript, 1939–40), p. 43ff.
11. Plato, *Phaedo*, trans. Henry Cary, p. 126.
12. Gigon, *Sokrates*, p. 116.
13. Ibid., p. 121.
14. Ibid., p. 126.
15. R. Allendy, *Le Symbolisme des Nombres*, 2d ed. (Paris, 1948), p. 41.
16. S. H. Diels, *Die Fragmente der Vorsokratiker*, 3d ed. (Berlin, 1912), vol. 1, p. 164; Hippol. ref. V. 8.
17. Jung, *Psychologische Interpretation von Kinderträumen*, p. 55.
18. Plato, *Crito* 50d–e. Cf. *The Works of Plato*, trans. Henry Cary, vol. 1, p. 40.
19. Jung, *Psychologische Interpretation von Kinderträumen*, p. 56ff.
20. See also C. G. Jung, *Aion* (Zurich: Rascher Verlag, 1951), p. 28ff.; and *Spring* (1950), p. 3ff.

21. Gigon, *Sokrates*, p. 111.
22. Plato, *Theatetus* 210c–d. Cf. *The Works of Plato*, trans. Cary, vol. 1, p. 455.
23. Jung, *Psychologische Interpretation von Kinderträumen*, p. 58ff.
24. Gigon, pp. 138–139.
25. Ibid., p. 107.
26. Cf. Karl Hoenn, *Artemis: Gestaltwandel einer Göttin* (Zurich: Artemis-Verlag, 1946).
27. Plato, *Phaedrus*, trans. J. Wright, in *Five Dialogues of Plato* (London: J. M. Dent, 1917), p. 209ff.
28. Plutarch, "De Genio Socratis," in *Opera Moralia;* and C. G. Jung, *English Seminar on the Interpretation of Visions*, vol. 1, p. 13ff.
29. Plato, *Apology* 23d. Cf. *The Works of Plato*, trans. Cary, vol. 1, p. 10.
30. Scholium to Plato's *Apology* 21e. Cf. also Gigon, *Sokrates*, p. 72.
31. Gigon, p. 117.
32. Homer, *The Iliad*, trans. Alexander Pope, book 9, p. 170ff.
33. Ibid., book 1, p. 13ff.
34. Ibid.
35. Ibid.
36. Plato, *Apology* 28b–d. Cf. *Four Socratic Dialogues of Plato*, trans. Benjamin Jowett (London: Oxford University Press, 1924), p. 72.
37. Johann Jakob Bachofen, *Versuch über die Gräbersymbolik der Alten*, 1st ed. (Basel, 1859), p. 73.
38. Ibid., p. 9; Philostratus = Heroikos, 1. 19.
39. Gigon, *Sokrates*, p. 167. Also related in Plato's *Apology*.
40. Gigon, p. 175.
41. Ibid., p. 176.
42. Ibid.
43. Ibid., p. 169.
44. Ibid., p. 166. Cf. also Plato's *Apology* 31d.
45. Gigon, p. 171.
46. C. G. Jung, *The Spirit Mercury*, trans. Gladys Phelan and Hildegard Nagel (New York: The Analytical Psychology Club of New York, 1953), p. 35.
47. Apuleius, *De Platone*, Lib. I, 1–2.
48. K. Kerényi, *Apollon* (Amsterdam: Pantheon, 1941).
49. Plutarch, "De Genio Socratis," 22ff. Cf. also C. A. Meier,

Antike Incubation und moderne Psychotherapie (Zurich: Rascher, 1949), p. 94ff.

50. Apuleius, *Liber de deo Socratis,* ed. P. Thomas (Teubner, 1908).

51. Plato, *The Symposium,* trans. Percy Bysshe Shelley, in *Five Dialogues of Plato,* p. 50ff.

52. Apuleius, *Liber de deo Socratis,* ed. P. Thomas, chap. 9, p. 17.

53. C. G. Jung, "Der Geist der Psychologie," in *Eranos-Jahrbuch* (Zurich: Rhein-Verlag, 1947), p. 460.

54. Ibid., p. 462.

The
Dreams of
Themistocles
and Hannibal

Translated by Elizabeth Welsh

I t might seem rather daring to try an interpretation of dreams which lie so far back in the past that we cannot ask the dreamer any questions. Naturally the interpretation of such historical dreams can only be a very tentative one. On the other hand dreams have—as we know—a compensatory function, and therefore, viewing them from this standpoint, it might be interesting to reconstruct the conscious situation in former times by studying contemporary dreams. We might be able to draw conclusions from the latter regarding the known historical situation and thus be in a position to answer certain questions which the historians, who only had the conscious material to work on, were not able to solve. We are incapable of knowing even our own conscious attitude per se, because we are too much involved and caught in it. We are only able to see our conscious attitude objectively through the reaction of the outer world on the one hand, and by seeing how our consciousness appears mirrored in the unconscious on the other. Similarly we can only see the conscious attitude of former times as it was mirrored in the unconscious of those times. Through knowing not only the conscious material by itself, but also its reflection in the unconscious, we shall perhaps be able to obtain a more complete picture of the situation in these former historical epochs.

A third reason for studying historical dreams lies in the fact that human nature in its deeper structural basis, does not change much within a few hundred years, so that we can look upon such historical dreams as still valuable case material through which it is possible to study some deeper typical reactions of the human psyche.

Most of the recorded dreams from antiquity contain only archetypal material.[1] We scarcely have any ordinary everyday dreams coming from earlier times, and most of the dreams are those of famous people. The only dreams we have of an ordinary man are in the diary of Ptolemaios, a *katochos*[a] in the Serapeum of Memphis. These form the only series of dreams in our possession, with the exception of the four great dreams of the Christian martyr Saint Perpetua.[2] We also have a collection of healing dreams from the sacred places of incubation.[3]

"Primitives," as Jung says,

> believe in two kinds of dreams; *ota* the great vision, big, meaningful and of collective importance, and *vudota*, the ordinary small dream. They usually deny having ordinary dreams, or if, after long efforts on your part, they admit such an occurrence, they say, "That is nothing. Everyone has that!" Great and important dreams are very rare and only a very big man has big dreams—chiefs, medicine men, people with mana. . . . Our usual prejudice against dreams—that they mean nothing—is probably just the old primitive tradition that the ordinary dreams are not worth noticing. . . .

> Perhaps the last traces of dreams of such public importance are to be found in Roman times. The daughter of a senator dreamt that a goddess appeared to her and reproached her for the fact that the temple was decaying through neglect, and asked that it should be rebuilt. So she went to the senate and reported the dream, and the senators decided to rebuild the temple.

> Another instance occurred in Athens when a famous poet[5] dreamt that a certain man had stolen a precious golden vessel from the temple of Hermes, and had hidden it in a certain place. He did not believe in dreams and the first time it happened he rejected it. But when it came a second and third time, he thought

---

[a] *Katochos* means "secluded prisoner of a god" or "possessed by a god."

that the gods were insisting and it might be true. So he went to the Aeropagus, the equivalent of the Roman Senate, and announced his dream. Then a search was made, the thief was found and the vessel restored.

African primitives now depend on the English to guide them, no longer on the medicine man's dream. The general opinion is that the medicine man or chief has no such dreams since the English have been in the country. They say the Commissioner knows everything now—the war boundaries, the boundaries of the fields, who has killed the sheep, etc. . . . This shows that the dream had formerly a social and political function, the leader getting his thoughts straight from heaven, guiding his people directly from his unconscious.[4]

Antiquity had the same attitude to dreams as the primitives and therefore only took note either of big dreams or of prognostic dreams which were reported if they were literally fulfilled. This is due no doubt to the special interest that was taken in them, but probably also to the fact that the people of that time were not able to realize things consciously and therefore generally lived the pattern of their fate naively. There are still modern examples of this; for instance, the life of the aviator and author Antoine de Saint Exupéry is the naive fulfillment of the archetypal *puer aeternus* tragedy; for where reflection is lacking, there is no freedom from inner fate.

Let me briefly review the life of Themistocles (514–449 B.C.). He was partly of Thracian origin, since only his father was Athenian; thus he was a *parvenu* in Attic culture, a man of little education. He was a genius, however, a natural personality; but he was also very ambitious and had quite a power complex. After the battle of Marathon, he is said to have wept for sheer rage at the glory of Miltiades. His great rival was the aristocrat Aristeides.

As is well known, Themistocles was the originator of naval expansion (as opposed to the infantry phalanx) and persuaded the Athenians to build two hundred ships with the money produced by the silver mines of Laurion. He likewise fortified the ports of the Piraeus against the imminent Persian invasion in the great war between Hellas and Persia. The Greek fleet opposing the Persians was commanded by a Spartan admiral, but at Salamis, through cunningly sending a messenger to Xerxes, Themistocles induced the latter to attack where it suited the Greeks, and it was thanks to this ruse that the battle was won. By his broad-minded policy in Athens, the repealing of the alien tax for instance, he did much to increase the power of the city.

After the victory of Salamis, however, Themistocles fell into an inflation. He even had a temple built to Artemis Euboulé ("of good counsel") next to his own house, with the result that his many rivals succeeded in having him ostracized by the people he had saved from the Persian onslaught. He was accused of bribery and treason. He fled to Argos, was pursued by the Spartans, escaped again to Corfu and from thence across to Asia Minor. Then Themistocles traveled at once to the Persian king (Xerxes or his son, Artaxerxes) and gave himself up. But such was the charm of his personality that the latter bestowed on him the town of Magnesia and two others with a handsome revenue, and he lived there with his family until the age of sixty-five. After his death a memorial was erected to him and he was worshiped as a god. On the coins which were struck to his memory he is depicted holding a dish over a slain bull. He appears, therefore, to have exercised the functions of a priest; but it is said in a later legend that he actually drank the blood of a bull, thus committing suicide, because he did not want to help the Persians against the Greeks.

Our point of interest takes us back to the time when Themistocles was flying from Corfu to Asia Minor, still uncertain if he should risk going straight into the camp of his former enemy. He was staying as a guest in the house of a rich Molossian chief who was also a friend of the Persians. The house priest, Olbios, after he had offered the evening sacrifice, said to Themistocles, "Let the night speak!" And it was there, in this desperate situation, trapped on all sides, that Themistocles had the following dream:

"A snake had wound itself up his body and had reached his throat. At that very moment it became an eagle that carried him away on its wings and deposited him on a herald's golden staff, and he was freed from his fear."

Without hesitation, Themistocles set out at once for the court of the king, disguised in women's clothes. He told the dream together with an oracle of Zeus which had encouraged him to take this step. Xerxes offered him two hundred talents, the price which had been put on his head, and then bestowed on him the three towns and the generous means of living already mentioned. The Persian court was naturally incensed at such a gesture, but Xerxes stuck to his decision to support his former enemy.

Interpretation of the Dream

The dream shows the typical structure of a drama,[6] and the first main motive is the snake which attacks the dreamer.

As the snake provides such extensive material for amplification, I will divide the material into some typical functions of the snake, which in antiquity was viewed

1. as an earth spirit (for example, the Midgard snake, the enemy of the higher gods in German mythology).

2. as the soul of the dead hero, a sepulchral demon (the snake coming out of the dead like worms; images of snakes on tombs with an egg as the symbol of rebirth[7]).

3. as *genius loci* (the *genius loci* of Athens, Cecrops living on the Acropolis; also the king Erechtheus, who as a babe was found in a box, entwined by snakes; and the half-snake king on the island of Salamis, Kychreus, who according to the legends appeared to encourage the Greeks at the battle of Salamis).

4. as a positive healing daimon (the snake of Aesculapius;[8] Aaron's rod).

5. as a mantic animal, inspiring the prophets (in fairy tales, eating a snake enables people to know the future or understand animals or birds. The seer Melampus had a snake on his shield).

6. as the mother in her negative aspect (the snake of Hecate, the feminine earth-demon; also the Python, the enemy of Apollo, or Echidna, half woman and half snake, or Gaea, the enemy of Hercules).

7. as a symbol of the spirit (Philo of Alexandria says of the snake that it is "the most spiritual animal imaginable because it is rapid as the pneuma, has neither feet nor hands, lives long and changes its skin, i.e., renews itself"). In alchemistic symbolism as in the Osiris and Sabazios mysteries it was the symbol of self-renewal.

The snake is such a paradoxical symbol because, as the enemy of the high gods and as earth demon, it represents the instinct, whereas, as "the most spiritual animal imaginable," it represents the spirit. To understand this I would like to refer to "On the Nature of the Psyche,"[9] in which Jung places psychic life between two poles: instinct, and the archetypal images and meanings of instinct, which are the elements of the spirit. The archetypal image and instinct are separated when we consider them theoretically, but they are united in the flow of life. It is this paradox that the snake represents; it is instinct and the spiritual meaning of the instinct as well. When the poles are united this is often represented through the winged snake, but there is also the widespread motif of the enmity between snake and eagle. The latter is beautifully illustrated in a Sumerian myth:

The eagle and the snake make an alliance before Shamash, the sun-god, to cooperate and hunt food together for their young. . . . The eagle, however, seeing the snake's young, decides to eat them and destroy the snake, and tears the latter with his talons. Thereupon the snake appeals to Shamash; following the god's advice, he catches the eagle by hiding in the carcass of an ox and tearing off his wings and talons, throws him into a pit. The eagle in turn appeals to Shamash to save his life, and Etana (man), who is seeking a plant to cure his wife, is sent down and, upon the eagle's promise to help him, takes him out of the pit. Etana then asks him for the plant, and the eagle flies up with him to heaven. When he reaches the gates of heaven, however, he can go no further and insists on descending; on the way down Etana perishes. (This myth was later applied to Alexander the Great, who is said to have harnessed a basket to two huge birds and induced them to carry him up in order that he might explore the vault of Heaven. . . . On the way up he met a bird-man who said to him, "Thou art ignorant of terrestrial things, why desirest thou to understand those of heaven? Return quickly to earth lest thou be the prey of these birds!")

This enmity of snake and eagle means that the opposites, spirit and instinct, can also fall apart, which is always a symptom of the need of reaching a state of higher consciousness. In Themistocles' dream the opposites, snake and bird, appear, one after the other, in the form of a typical enantiodromia.

In the case of Themistocles, we must emphasize the motif of the *genius loci;* he has a vocation for his country, he is "called" by fate, by the genius of Athens; this is the motif of the superpersonal task. A collective spiritual power seizes upon his individual existence and drives him into a collective role. As the snake winds itself up around him, so is he driven by his genius, he is no longer its master, hence his inflation; he has become inhuman. Had he remained in the grasp of the snake he might have become insane or criminal. But as it touches his head the snake turns into an eagle. The eagle also, like the snake, has many aspects. As a creature of the air, it is a symbol of the spirit. In a Melanesian myth, for instance, the wizard sends his soul forth for information in the form of an eagle. The Apache Indians believe that divine spirits dwell in the eagle. Eagles' feathers are prized for ritual purposes. With us it is the bird of Saint John, because as the church fathers say, he had the power of contemplating divine glory.

The eagle often personifies the sun and, like the snake, the principle of self-renewal. In an ancient Sumerian myth, the eagle is the sun itself, rising or at its height. According to ancient myths it flies up to the sun until its feathers burn and fall off, then it falls down to the earth again and grows new feathers and becomes young again like the phoenix.

It is a messenger and a bringer of salvation. In an Iranian myth, the eagle brings the gift of fire and is a messenger between man and the higher powers. The Indians believe that the eagle is sent down as a shaman to counteract evil deeds and bad spirits. In Greece it is the messenger of Zeus.

It is a symbol of power and leadership. The eagle is often the leader of Indian tribes. In the migration myth of the Aztecs, where an eagle appeared perching on a cactus they founded a city. The Roman legions liked to choose their winter quarters where they found an eagle's nest. The Roman emperor carried a scepter on the top of which stood an eagle. Jung says:

> . . . the eagle soars high, it is near the sun, it is the sun, marvelous, the bird of light, it is the very high thought, the great enthusiasm. For instance, when Ganymede, the messenger of Zeus, is lifted up by the eagle to Olympian heights, it is the genius and enthusiasm of youth that seizes and carries him up to the heights of the gods. So one could say it was a spiritual, uplifting power. . . . That is what the spirit can do—spiritual excitement, spiritual enthusiasm; suddenly, after having hovered over a crowd for a while, the spirit picks somebody out and lifts him up on high. And the serpent would be "la force terrestre."[10]

In the dream of Themistocles it is when the snake touches his face that it turns into an eagle. The face is the main part of the head, and the head is the seat of the mental functions, the seat of awareness. The functions of sensations are mostly localized in the face; sight, smell, hearing and taste. According to the alchemists the head represents the sphere of heaven in the microcosm of man. If the snake, which up to now was a symbol of instinctive driving forces coming from below, touches the face, and especially the chin, it means that these blind driving forces have now become conscious and that they now enter the field of awareness. This also means that its dynamic finds an expression through the mouth, an allusion perhaps to Themistocles' demagogic power. But even so, Themistocles is still possessed, the eagle carries him far away. The transformation of the snake into the eagle probably means his "great plans": his power drive and the enthusiasm which carries him. He himself as a human being, however, is completely helpless, therefore his feeling of terror. In reality he was in a most difficult situation: he had inwardly lost every contact with the earth and also he actually had lost his home town, his own ground; he was always among foreigners, always in danger. Every major inflation causes such a loss of reality; Themistocles ignored the psyche of his fellow men.

Then we come to the lysis of the dream with the appearance of the golden staff. The staff means the demarcation of a temenos, the objective lead that can rule in judgment; it is an instrument of order; a staff is used to keep cattle in order, and to the same end kings hold a scepter and medicine men carry staffs. Honorius of Autun called the bishop's staff the "auctoritas doctrinae." As the king's scepter and the Roman fasces, the staff is a symbol of power, the judgment which determines the life and death of citizens. To announce festivals among the tribes, the Eskimos sent out heralds carrying feathered staffs, the bearing of which characterized them as spiritual shepherds. The staff, or wand, of Hermes was the instrument by which he lulled people to sleep or awakened them and which he also used to lead the dead. The herald's wand also means certain laws which are above conflict, "au-dessus de la mêlée." It is the mediator between the opposites and carries the germ of the union. Therefore the heralds with their staffs were sacrosanct in antiquity.

The solution of our dream consists in the fact that Themistocles suddenly stands on the staff, which represents a transformed aspect of his former power-genius and power drive. It is the last and most solid form of it. In the symbol of the staff the power drive is internalized and has become inner authority; now he is carried by his inner personality between the opposites. He must rely on inner guidance and trust that which threatens him, his own enemy. Themistocles actually did this in the outer world when he quoted the voice of the dream to the Persian king. He had to rely completely on the other side, that is, the unconscious—therefore the gods helped him.

The staff is the third form of the snake and the eagle. In alchemy the snake is the first form of the transforming substance, as ouroboros, dragon, and so on. Then comes the eagle or other birds as the first sublimated form of the same substance, and in the end we have the gold as the incorruptible goal. When we consider these alchemistic parallels we might assume that the staff is identical with the eagle and snake, but that which was once possession by passion and power drive has now been crystallized into an inner firmness. We could therefore say that the dream says to Themistocles: "Now you are trapped and carried away off the ground. But stand on what you are; your own inner basis, then you will be secure." But we must realize that a herald's staff is a very small basis to stand upon, and indeed, at the age of thirty-five Themistocles lost the whole field of collective outer activity! This was an incredible change in his life: henceforth he was to lead a retired life with his wife and three sons, probably taking over certain religious functions as a priest in his new country.

I would like to compare this drama in Themistocles' life with a similar situation which, however, took a tragic turn and did not lead to such a positive solution, namely, with the famous dream of Hannibal, the great leader of Carthage against the Romans. He was a great military genius and exceedingly loved by his legions. Let us first briefly review his life.

The Life of Hannibal (247–183 B.C.)

Hannibal was actually brought up in the atmosphere of his father Hamilcar's hatred of the Romans. When he was nine years old, his father made him swear a solemn oath in the temple of Baal against the Romans; and at an early age he was taken along on his father's campaigns to Spain and thus separated from his mother.

At that time there was a pact between the two great powers of Carthage and Rome according to which neither would touch the possessions of *socii* of the other south and north of the Ebro respectively. Saguntum, however, was not mentioned in it. Nevertheless, by attacking Saguntum Hannibal was morally responsible for starting the war, true to the oath he had sworn to his father. His famous crossing of the Alps with his elephants is well known. On his way through the Apennines, crossing a swamp, he lost a great number of men and contracted a disease of the eyes through which he practically lost the sight of one eye. After the surprise victory of Cannae, he failed to attack Rome immediately, as his cavalry leader, Maharbal, was anxious to do, preferring to stop and consider, and thus lost his chance. Rome had time to strengthen her defenses, and fortune then turned against him. Scipio went to Africa, and Hannibal was beaten at the battle of Zama. Although defeated, he was made suffete of Carthage, but he was accused of intriguing and fled to Antiochus IV of Syria and again made war on Rome. Hannibal was again beaten and again fled, this time to King Prusias of Bithynia. But there he was betrayed again and on the point of being arrested committed suicide by taking poison.

Now Cicero records in his writing *De Divinatione* the following dream of Hannibal:

The Dream of Hannibal[11]

Coelius[12] related that when Hannibal had taken Saguntum he dreamed that he was summoned to a council of the gods; and that when he arrived there Jupiter commanded him to carry the war into Italy; and one of the deities in the council was appointed to be his conductor in the enterprise. He therefore began his march under the direction of his divine protector, who enjoined him not to look behind him. Hannibal, however, could not keep long in his obedience, but yielded to a great desire to look back, when he immediately beheld a huge and terrible monster, like a serpent, which, whenever it advanced, destroyed all trees and shrubs and buildings. Marveling at this, he inquired of the god what this monster might mean, and the god replied that it signified the desolation of Italy, and commanded him to advance without delay and not to concern himself with the evils that lay behind him in his rear.

Later on in his campaign, Hannibal had a second, less important dream; Cicero's text reads:

Coelius relates that Hannibal, wishing to remove a golden column from the temple of Juno Lacinia, and not knowing whether it was gold or merely gilt, bored a hole in it; and as he found it solid, he determined to take it away. The following night Juno appeared to him in a dream and warned him against doing so, and threatened him that if he did she would take care that he should lose the eye with which he could see well (the only one left). . . . Thereupon he restored the gold which he had abstracted from the column in boring it.

What is immediately striking about the first dream is that the Roman father of the gods, Jupiter, commands Hannibal in the council of the Olympian gods. It is not his own Phoenician god Baal, as one would expect, so this seems to be a trap. Gods, as we know, are personifications of archetypes. If, therefore, the Roman gods give him advice it means that unconsciously Hannibal recognizes them as his gods rather than his own god. His unconscious personality worships the Roman gods, or the effective archetypes appear to him in the Roman sphere, in the enemy's camp.

That the name of Jupiter is not merely "interpretatio Romana" (i.e., the use of the name Jupiter to mean Baal) is proved by the fact that the text mentions a council of gods. The Carthaginian Baal was the prince consort of Ishtar, not a member of a council of gods. Moreover, he was a chthonic god of fertility, and his name would rather have been translated into Latin as Pluto, the Roman god of the underworld, with whom he has the closest affinities. In addition, the second dream introduces the Roman mother-goddess Juno, as is proven by her surname Lacinia (= Lucina). This would confirm the fact that the archetypes, or Hannibal's unconscious, appear in Roman form. His unconscious was projected on to the Romans. Thus Hannibal had indeed lost his roots: he had left Carthage at the age of nine—and Carthage itself was a cosmopolitan city with a very mixed population. Moreover, he was separated from his mother, and it is generally the mother who transmits the tradition of the land to her children.

The first sentence of the dream already shows the coming catastrophe: "Carry the war into Italy." This was a great risk.

The strength of the Carthaginians lay in their fleet. Hannibal's incredible strategy was of Greek tradition, which he adopted as the Romans had done. He was misled into fighting the Romans with their own weapons, instead of insisting on naval warfare, where the Romans were weak. He had unconsciously projected his highest values, investing them in Italy, so he was fascinated by the latter country. It was interesting to observe the same phenomenon, the overvaluing of the enemy, in the dreams of people in both England and Germany before World War II.

Hannibal did not have his own people behind him. (Carthage was one of the independent colonies, not the "Imperium.") His aim was pure revenge. He had no other object: he was carried away by the collective aim. Later he claimed to be the defender of Greek culture. He had no roots, either in his own being or in his nation, so he was doomed to failure.

Who, we must now ask, is the "bright youth" (as he is called in Livy's text) who conducted Hannibal? He belongs to the same type as Mercury, or the *puer aeternus,* a typical psychopomp-figure. He might also be called Hannibal's genius. The Roman genius was always experienced outside; the inspiring factor was projected and autonomous. In antiquity, the ego-consciousness of man was still too weak to realize the inner factors directly; like the primitives, he saw them personified outside. Thus the genius meant the core of the vital unconscious personality.

The genius told Hannibal that he must not look back. This is the motif in the mythologem of Orpheus leading Eurydice out of Hades, and that of Lot's wife escaping from the city of destruction. In Lot's wife's case, she dared not look back because she could not stand the sight of the dark, revengeful side of God. In the case of Orpheus, he is in a state where the anima, Eurydice, having been poisoned, would poison him too, that is, tempt him and pull him into the land of the dead. Another justification for this taboo may be that the light of consciousness sometimes interrupts a process of inner development.[13]

The snake here is the negative side of the Hermes-genius

and also Hannibal's own shadow. Probably the latter is forbidden to see it on account of his weakness. He is incapable of seeing his own dual aspect and would have broken down if he did see it.

In the case of Themistocles, as we remember, the dark side came first: he lived a wild life as a young man, and his light side developed organically out of dark roots; whereas Hannibal became cut off from his dark side in early youth.

Hannibal's natural curiosity now made him turn, and he beheld the huge and terrible monster. The snake, according to Jung, is the dark crowd-soul within. Hannibal was carried by a political, collective aim, therefore there was the danger of his being merely the instrument of a collective tendency. This reveals a certain weakness in his personality. Hitler also, for instance, was wholly carried by collective aims and means. There was nothing left of the private person. That was the drawback of the genius of Hannibal—and the only cure would have been voluntary loneliness. But Hannibal never retired as Themistocles did, never stopped to question the meaning of his dream. The "bright youth" prophesied the ruin of Italy, and this proved to be objectively true: the south of Italy was laid waste; three hundred thousand men were lost through the war, four hundred towns and villages were destroyed, there were no peasants left, the Romans lost the reservoir of the peasant population. But why does the "bright youth" not allow Hannibal to see the monster? Hannibal was unconsciously in love with, or fascinated by, the Roman Empire. There was no sense in destroying it; it would have been far better to conquer it. As this fact of being actually led by Roman divine forces is shown by the unconscious, it is clear that he did not realize it consciously. He was caught in an illusion: that of the chivalrous idea of war (just as Napoleon spoke of himself as the greatest fighter in the cause of peace!).

The bright youth is, according to Jung,[14] a variation of the archetype of the shepherd, like Orpheus, Poimandres, or the Indian god Krishna. He is a god who leads the herd of mankind. To be fascinated by him means that Hannibal longs to be a god, but if he does this he also constellates the shadow of this god, the serpent, a great destructive monster. We may conclude, says Jung, that he had a very positive idea of himself, probably as a sort of savior of his own people, and he did not realize that he was also a terrible monster. But that is what often happens to people who do not see the shadow. They think they only mean the best for their nation or for the whole world, never reckoning with the fact of what they actually produce! . . . The monster stands also for the crowd within, the collective unconscious, the crowd soul of man,[15] against which one can only stand *if one does not sell one's soul to an organization and has the courage to stand completely alone.* According to this dream, Hannibal obviously could not do this, but the golden staff of Themistocles' dream means precisely that— the individual solitude.

Now in Hannibal's second dream of the golden column, Juno threatens Hannibal with the loss of the one eye remaining to him. The unconscious speaks in the dream as a Roman goddess, and he obeys at once. Normally he was not in the habit of obeying. When he was at the court of Anthiochus IV, for example, a sacrifice was offered up, and the haruspex (diviner) declared that the entrails of the calf prophesied defeat. Hannibal, far from being submissive, exclaimed: "Do you trust the entrails of a calf rather than my own ability?" There he was inflated. This shows how much it meant for him to obey Juno and confirms once again that his inner values were projected on the Roman gods. When he was crossing the Apennines with his armies, in the plain of the Arno they came upon a swamp where Hannibal lost his last elephant, and there he developed an inflammation and lost one eye. Juno must have had something to do with the destruction of this first eye also. The snake is among other things also a personification of the swamp, so Juno must somehow be connected with the huge snake of the first dream too.

The one eye is the motif of the one-sided viewpoint. Such accidents are, as we know, symbolical of the standpoint of the victim; maimed hands, for instance, in which the right hand stands for acting from the point of view of consciousness. The snake motif is also connected with the female side, from which

Hannibal was unnaturally torn away at the age of nine. The
Spanish woman whom he married does not appear to have
counted for much in his life. He lived entirely for his military
assignments and was possessed by his aim. Therefore the
feminine principle had become merged with the collective
unconscious (the snake). He was threatened by Juno Lacinia,
the protectress in childbirth. Lacinia is derived from *lux* = light:
she helped the child into the light—and was the protectress of
the eyebrows. Hannibal never came to terms with the anima,
the feminine principle in himself. Themistocles, on the other
hand, as we know, had a wife who followed him into exile,
and lived a personal life. He was capable of integrating the
"other side" and with it the feminine side. This is a typical
crisis in the life of very masculine powerful men, that they fall
short when they have to go through this transformation. Some
Indian tribes try to help by having such a man wear women's
clothes in the second half of life. It also represents the turn
from action to wisdom, from leadership to retirement, seclusion, and a religious attitude toward life. Whereas Hannibal's
dream and life ended tragically, the dream of Thermistocles
has a solution: he comes to stand upon a golden staff.

The gold of the staff in the dream means the indestructible,
incorruptible, that is, magic value. Gold is related to the sun
principle, to consciousness beyond destruction. The fact that
Themistocles stands on the staff and not on the earth means
that he does not discover the earth outside (this would only
have been an enantiodromia, whereas his was a real transformation transcending the opposites); the power which gripped
him turned into an inner earth, an inner basis, but he can no
longer move about much outwardly. He understood this inner
task and abandoned all outer power and activities.

It might be interesting to compare the two modes of interpretation; namely, how people looked at dreams in the past
and how we see them now.

In antiquity they would have interpreted the snake as the
daimon or god of Athens gripping the dreamer—as a divine
power. The eagle would probably have been seen as the symbol

of his high career; and the golden staff as the money and safety which he got at the end of his life.

Today we would rather say that an instinctive impulse carries the dreamer into a collective role and leads to an inflation and spiritual exaltation which endangers his human life, but that this can still be transformed into an increase of consciousness leading to the process of individuation.

We emphasize the psychic function of the dream, whereas the Greeks emphasized the prophetic function. One sees how in antiquity men were little aware of their soul. It needed our development via Christianity to make us aware of the psychic factor and thus it is only now that we can understand these dreams as an inner process. They illustrate, it seems to me, a very typical and important turning point in the life of these two great men and beyond that throw light on some classical aspects of the process of individuation as we know it today.

Notes

1. The main sources are Artemidorus, *Oneirokritika*; Cicero, *De Divinatione*; Synesius, *De Insomniis*; Plutarch's and Suetonius's *Lives* provide most of the source material of dreams in Greek and Roman times.
2. This series of visions I have treated fully in *The Passion of Perpetua* (Irving, Tex.: Spring Publications, 1979).
3. See C. A. Meier, *Antike Incubation und Moderne Psychotherapie* (Zurich: Rascher, 1949).
4. *English Seminar on Dream Analysis,* vol. 1, Autumn 1928, p. 2.
5. Sophocles.
6. a. Time and place: the present.
   b. Dramatis personae: Themistocles, snake, eagle, staff.
   c. Exposition: snake winding itself up to his throat.
   d. Peripeteia: eagle carries him away—feeling of fear.
   e. Lysis: he is put down on the herald's golden staff—his fear vanishes.
7. Cf. E. Küster, *Die Schlange in der griechischen Kunst und Religion* (Giessen, 1913), p. 36ff.
8. Cf. Meier, *Antike Incubation*.
9. C. G. Jung, *CW* 8.

10. *English Seminar on Psychological Analysis of Nietzsche's Zarathustra,* part 1, Spring 1934 (Zürich: multigraphed typescript), p. 19.
11. The sources I have used are Cicero, *De Divinatione* 1.24 (Chicago: University of Chicago Press, 1949), and the translation in F. Seafield, *The Literature and Curiosities of Dreams* (London, 1865), vol. 11, p. 71f.
12. Coelius is Cicero's source on this subject.
13. This is the motif of Psyche throwing the candlelight on her divine husband, Amor, in defiance of his wish. Here, therefore, consciousness is excluded because it is too bright. In analysis we endeavor to find concepts by which the unconscious can be adequately expressed, but sometimes these may kill growth in the psyche by pulling out something which is not yet ready for the light.
14. *Seminar on Zarathustra,* vol. 9, Spring 1938, p. 75. See also ibid., vol. 10, p. 112.
15. Ibid.

Monica,
Mother of
Saint Augustine

Translated by Emmanuel Xipolitas Kennedy and Vernon Brooks

During the years that Saint Augustine was resisting his mother's persistent and relentless entreaties to give up his dissolute life and be baptized (their quarrels were so venomous they could not even eat at the same table), Monica, the mother, had the following dream which Augustine reports in his *Confessions*:

> She saw herself standing on a wooden rule and a youth all radiant coming to her cheerful and smiling upon her, whereas she was grieving and heavy with her grief. He asked her—not to learn from her, but as is the way of visions, to teach her—the causes of her sorrow and the tears she daily shed. She replied that she was mourning for the loss of my soul. He commanded her to be at peace and told her to observe carefully and she would see that where she was, there was I also. She looked, and saw me standing alongside her on the same rule.

Augustine continues, "When she told me her vision and I tried to interpret it to mean that she must not despair of one day being as I was, she answered without an instant's hesitation: 'No. For it was not said to me where he is, you are, but where you are, he is.' "[1] Augustine adds that at the time of the dream he was more deeply moved by her answer than he was by the dream-vision itself.

The Life of Saint Augustine (A.D. 354–430)

Saint Augustine was born in the town of Tagaste in the province of Numidia, North Africa. His father, Patricius, was a pagan who is supposed to have been converted in later life to Christianity. However, at the time Augustine was living at home, Patricius, a very temperamental man, was still a fanatical pagan.

So Augustine grew up in a religiously divided household. He inherited the passionate nature of his father. He went when he was twelve to the grammar school in Madaura and five years later to Carthage, where he became a teacher of rhetoric and wrote Latin in a rhetorical style. At nineteen he read Cicero's *Hortensius* and grew increasingly interested in philosophical and religious questions. He became a follower (even a "Hearer") of the Manichaeans, thanks to the influence of their elegant orator and leader, Faustus, bishop of Milevis. Later he returned to Tagaste and worked there as a teacher. His mother made life unbearable for him, however, for he did not want to have to listen to her arguments about being converted to Christianity; she made such fearful scenes with him that even a bishop she consulted reprimanded her for her temper. It was at this time that Monica had the dream which was realized in reality some eleven years later. At the time, however, Augustine had not yet been converted. He went to Rome, where the teachings of the Manichaeans disappointed him more and more. He was happy, therefore, when he received a teaching appointment in Milan in 384 and as a result was separated from the Manichaeans. During this period he studied Neoplatonic texts for the most part.

Manichaeism is a dualistic religious system. Its founder, Mani, was from a Persian or Jewish family; it is said of him that he was the son or even the slave of a widow from whom he stole the Books of Wisdom. Manichaeism has links with Buddhism and contains in its teachings Indian, Zoroastrian, Babylonian, and Syrian elements. The sect spread as far afield as India and China.

Manichaeism taught the existence of two gods in two

realms, a light and a dark universe, which were completely separated from each other. The good god had various messengers, of whom Christ was one, but the principal redeemer was Mani. The son of darkness was Ahriman. The first man, Adam, fell into darkness instead of fighting against it and left his weapons (which consisted of his five sons) in the darkness. In this way light and darkness were entangled. Then God created the real world as a machine designed to liberate the light sparks (the zodiacal wheel). The individual human being is deceived by the Devil, but there are light particles within him and his task is to release them. The solution lies in the restoration of the light sparks and in the complete separation of light from darkness, at which time the world will be destroyed by fire.

As in the majority of Gnostic systems, salvation in Manichaeism depends on gnosis. The word *gnosis* does not mean only "knowledge," but also a personal experience of God. The Manichaeans compare this experience with awakening in darkness: the redeemer calls out and the soul answers; the soul can only be redeemed within itself. Therefore salvation does not depend so much on ritual, although ritual also plays an important role; the principal inner experience is gnosis. Manichaeism is a religion of struggle and self-control. The Manichaeans were vegetarians and regarded plants and vegetables, including melons and cucumbers, as an especially favorable diet.

This dualistic view of God satisfies the intellect to a certain extent, for it accounts for the existence of evil. But for feeling, this teaching, with its absolute condemnation of the world, is very discouraging; it is too pessimistic. Besides, feeling resists the idea of two gods, for feeling would like to experience God as an ultimate oneness or unity. Probably these were the facts which lay behind Augustine's disappointment with Manichaeism.

The concept of the "one God," as mentioned above, was brought nearer to Augustine through Neoplatonism, which is closer to Christian theological doctrine; it taught the existence of "one good God" but denied the existence of evil (which, according to Augustine's later formulation of the problem, is merely a *privatio boni*) and thus emphasized only the light side of God. As long as Augustine devoted himself to Neoplatonism he still acted out of his superior psychic function—intellectual thinking—although he had embraced a holistic viewpoint which made it possible for the inferior function to break into consciousness.

Although Augustine had approached the Christian standpoint intellectually, through his acceptance of Neoplatonism, he was still depressed and unsatisfied. A breakthrough of his inferior function was necessary—an event which can occur but which cannot be brought about by one's will. An inner psychic experience is necessary. In Milan Augustine met with Ambrose, the great statesman and patrician bishop, and studied the Bible with his lifelong friend Alypius. However, he was unable to accept the Holy Scriptures because, from his very intellectual standpoint, they were contrary to all logic. Then Ambrose taught him the method of allegorical interpretation and thus opened the door for him to the possibility of reading the Bible with his intellect.

Despite the fact that Augustine thus became gradually closer to the Christian doctrines with his intellect, there was still something of an unconscious barrier in him to becoming a Christian. According to Jung, a conversion to Christianity—on the part of those few exceptional individuals who genuinely strove to follow Christ's example—consisted in the sacrifice of the superior function. Jung illustrates this with the examples of Tertullian and Origen and mentions that Augustine was similar to the latter.[2] Saint Augustine, too, had to sacrifice his intellect. We must therefore ask ourselves where his feelings were blocked. They were probably still tied to his mother, and as a result he never had a serious relationship with another woman.

In Carthage Augustine lived a normal sensual life. He sired an illegitimate son whom he called Adeodatus, and after the birth of the child he sent the mother away. But he acquired another female companion of the same questionable character. The problem of chastity, however, troubled him more and more (i.e., psychologically he wanted to remain faithful to the mother-image), but he could not make up his mind to give up his associations with "inferior" women.

However, the inner tension between his impulse and his proud intellect which made it possible for him to resist the former became manifestly more urgent, until he could no longer reject the inner voice. He was sitting one evening with Alypius, who was aware of the bitter conflict going on in Augustine, when a sudden outburst of tears on the part of the latter forced him to withdraw from his friend's company. Sobbing, Augustine fled to the garden and flung himself down beneath a fig tree. There he heard the voice of a child saying, "Tolle lege, tolle lege!" ("Take it and read, take it and read!"). Augustine ran back to Alypius, who at that moment was reading the Epistles of Paul. Augustine seized the Bible, opened it to Romans 13:13f and read silently: ". . . not in reveling and drunkenness, not in immorality and wantonness, not in strife and envying; But put ye on the Lord Jesus Christ, and make not provision for the flesh, to fulfill its lusts." In his description of this event in the *Confessions*, Augustine says, "In that instant, with the very ending of the sentence, it was as though a light of utter confidence shone in all my heart, and all the darkness of uncertainty vanished away." And he adds, "For You converted me to Yourself so that I no longer sought a wife nor any of this world's promises, but stood upon that same rule of faith in which You had shown me to her so many years before."[3]

Since at that time he was suffering from some illness of the chest which made it impossible to work, he gave up his teaching position before the beginning of the Easter holidays and retired with some friends to a country villa, loaned him by a friend, at Cassiciacum, near Milan. The following Easter he was baptized, together with his son and Alypius. His mother joined them at Cassiciacum and was joyful over the fulfillment of her prayers. She died at Ostia, as they were getting ready to embark for Africa.

Augustine remained in Rome until 388, when he returned to Africa, where presumably his son died shortly thereafter. He led a monastic life in the community of Hippo (in Proconsular

Africa) and became its bishop in the year 395. He spent his life in conflict and confrontation, especially with the Manichaeans, the dogmatists, and with Pelagius, an advocate of "original sin." Then Augustine wrote *The City of God*. One of his last works, *On the Trinity*, is enormously interesting psychologically, for in it he compares the hypostasis of the Trinity with psychic phenomena and processes. His exegesis of Genesis is symbolically of great importance. It is as if, in this last phase of his life, his pugnacious behavior had finally made way for a more mature and complete understanding of Christian truths.

Saint Augustine died at the age of seventy-six, in 430, the year the Vandals besieged Hippo.

Interpretation of the Dream

Our attention should first be directed to the fact that *Augustine's mother is standing on the carpenter's rule*. The rule is used for the most part to draw a simple line or a rectangle. It recalls Joseph's profession—in mythology one of the oldest of trades. Craftwork represents mankind's first attempt to subdue nature, hence in general it stands symbolically for an essential activity leading to a higher awareness. Since creation myths are symbolic representations of the origin of human consciousness, it is not surprising that certain handicraft arts are often mentioned in them. Thus, in Egypt the potter-god makes the world, in India it is the smith-god, and the carpenter also appears in India in the role of the demiurge (Rigveda). Whereas the Holy Spirit is the spiritual father of Jesus, Joseph is, so to speak, his darker, demiurgic father. The rule is the instrument with which one makes things straight. Thus, for example, in the commentary to the *I Ching* it is said, "The symbol of heaven is the circle, and that of earth . . . a straight line."[4] In Latin *regula* ("rule") also means "canon," that is, the canonical books of the Holy Scriptures, as opposed to the Apocrypha.

However, there is something unusual in our dream. Instead of holding the rule in her hands, Monica *stands* on it. She uses it in the wrong way. The instrument probably represents her Christian animus convictions; those convictions are a correct perception of the circumstances but one which Monica cannot deal with as a woman would who employs her animus consciously, for instance in creative work. When Monica wanted to convince others, she used her animus in the wrong way, that is, stubbornly and willfully. The bishop recognized this and was aware of her rigid unchristian attitude, which made it impossible to discuss anything with her. Monica should have worked harder toward a better realization of her own standpoint; she would then have been able to explain it to others instead of trying to force it upon them. Her convictions were those of an animus possession coming from the collective unconscious. Women usually accept any new spirit of the times more quickly than men, and accept it with their animus, which is a *logos spermatikos*, because frequently they are less skeptical. That is why they are often carriers of new religious movements (for instance, the Dionysian mysteries, Saint Perpetua,[5] and the like). But then it is often an unaccountable, fanatic conviction which possesses them. We must consider Monica's situation. She was the only Christian in her family, so there was no instinctive, intimate atmosphere to support her belief. Her relation to her husband was of no help. When a marriage is as unhappy as hers, it is natural for a mother to concentrate quite involuntarily and far too intensely on her son. Augustine, however, was no weak mother's boy; he resisted her, and so in her dream she received a sharp admonition not to worry about him; otherwise she would have castrated him. This points to the animus problem of mothers who insist on forcing their opinions on their sons.

Then the radiant youth asks Monica, "Why do you complain?" He says this so that she may pause, reflect, and recognize what she is doing. The youth is, in a certain way, the messenger of God. Psychologically, he must also be an inner figure in Monica, pointing, since he is young, to a new spiritual attitude. In this sense he is the double of her son; he is what Augustine should become, according to her wishes; she would like to impose this animus onto him. The fact that the youth appears as a figure separate from her son means that she needs to become conscious of what she is projecting. He is *bright*, which indicates his function of *enlightenment*. Wherever an a priori conviction prevails, it is not assimilated; a long step-by-step development is needed before it can be actualized in a human way. This is the purpose of the appearance of the youth; he teaches the correct, human attitude. An allusion to this was initially present in the motif of the rule, which is a human instrument, not a product of nature. The spirit could just as well have been symbolized by wind, for instance, or by an eagle.

The rule is an instrument for measuring, which is also a human function (*anthropos panton metron*, "man is the measure of all things"). We find the idea of a Christian measure in Paul's Epistle to the Ephesians (4:13): "Till we all come in the unity of the faith and of the knowledge of the Son of God, unto a perfect man, unto the measure of the stature of the fullness of Christ." The body of Christ is regarded here as an ideal measure for man; he is the community of believers. A reference to measure appears again in Scripture, in the Wisdom of Solomon (11:20), where it is said of the creator, "You have set all things in order by measure and number and weight." Augustine writes in his commentary on this verse that it means "in God Himself. . . . He, who is number without number, weight without weight, measure without measure."[6] Alanus ab Insulis says that numbers are ideas or patterns in the spirit of God.[7] The archetypes, which are numbers, are contained in the *sapientia dei*, the wisdom of God. There are also interesting alchemical speculations concerning weighing and measuring. Albertus Magnus, in the *Paradisus Animae*, declares that measure is attributed to God, number to the Son, and weight to the Holy Spirit; we ought therefore to live our lives according to the right measure.

The problem of "weight and measure" appears also in psychological work. This motif often alludes to one of the difficult problems in analysis, namely the extent to which a dream motif should be taken concretely and/or the extent to which it should be taken symbolically. There is no rule for that. If, for instance, someone dreams that he is insulted by or insults someone who personifies the shadow, one does not know how far that person represents the inner shadow or to what extent the dreamer—taken concretely—should avoid the real person. This is exactly a problem of weight and measure. Jung says that one must *feel* one's way into a dream; it is a question of *feeling*, which is a weighing and valuing function, a feelinglike distribution of weight and measure. The meaning of a dream is never found by logic alone.

An Arabic alchemical text states that numbers are the bond between body and soul; this alludes again to the above-mentioned problem of the concrete and symbolic (that is, psychic) aspects of every dream image.

This accords with Monica's situation. In her zeal to convert her son she has lost every measure. The light youth says, "Be at peace, be careful and observe where you are, and you will find that your son will be there too." He leads her to a more introverted, more conscious attitude and in doing so means to say to her, "Stop quarreling, for when you quarrel you just lose libido, your energy simply runs away. You must stop all that for your own sake, if you don't want to lose your son." That is why the angel stresses the fact that he is already close to her, which means that she will lose him if she tries too hard.

The dream informs her that her son is standing beside her; *that is the lysis of the dream.* It is the direct opposite of the facts as she knows them in reality. Since the unconscious is not restricted to time, one can also say that it is as if his conversion has already taken place. The dream would then simply be prophetic (that is, literally true). However, I do not believe that the motif only foresees a future event, that of Augustine's conversion. Rather, it points to deeper reasons and connections. In order to discover them I must refer to something I have already suggested, namely that conversion to Christianity is a special psychic transformation. In Tertullian and Origen we see that this transformation involves the *sacrifice of the superior function.* Tertullian sacrificed his intellect, thereby gaining depths of feeling through which he arrived at his famous paradoxical view of Christ. Origen, on the other hand, through self-castration, sacrificed his extraversion, his relation to the outer world, and won the wealth of Gnostic thinking.[8]

Augustine, from the point of view of typology, resembled Tertullian; until the time of his conversion he was a thinking type. The inferiority of his feeling is indicated by the licentious life he had previously led. His feeling was in the dark, until it emerged along with the violent breakthrough of his inferior function. His genuine feeling, which until then had been tied to his mother, now turned to Christ and the church. Since Augustine was an introvert, his fourth function had of necessity to be of an extraverted character and therefore it moved toward outer objects, that is, to the visible Roman Catholic church. This also explains, retrospectively, why he did not like the Manichaean denial of the world. At the same time the Catholic church offered a monistic system to the undifferentiated feeling function. Only differentiated thinking and feeling can endure the paradox, whereas inferior feeling wishes to find absolute love or absolute faith. For that reason the opposites cannot be accepted consciously through the latter. All of Roman Catholic teaching is in opposition to Manichaeism, for it denies dualism and defines God as a *summum bonum*, as the highest good. From where then does evil come? This is the difficult question, for which Manichaeism can provide a more satisfactory answer. If God is the highest good, where then is evil? It is sometimes explained as the result of man's disobedience, or the rebellion of the angels, or Satan's fall. So Augustine and Basilius Magnus, among others, regarded evil as something insubstantial, a mere *privatio boni*. For Augustine the solution was a feeling matter; what is emphasized is that it is man's task to follow the good. This is typical of the optimism of early Christianity. It was the impulse of a movement which wanted to raise man above the dark world of antiquity. With Saint Augustine the breakthrough of his feeling function was the solution. The inferior function, whatever it may be, contains the highest value, although it is experienced as the greatest handicap.

Augustine's new feeling attitude toward the Christian church stands opposed to the fact that he was first a fanatic opponent of the church. For an intellectual introvert, as he was, it meant first a complete about-face. This is his *imitatio Christi*. After

Ambrose's allegoric instruction the restless pace began, until the inferior function broke through with great emotion; feeling overwhelmed him through its newness. Until then, as we have seen, his feeling had been hidden in the mother; this is typical for a mother's son, and when feeling is in the keeping of the mother then all other women are present only for a vulgar biological affair. His intellect runs around alone. It is interesting that Augustine's mother died so quickly after his conversion; had she become superfluous now that his feeling had found a higher mother image—the *Ecclesia?*

The mother-complex thread runs through the lives of many important men, giving them an inner feminine attitude which leaves them open to the contents of the unconscious. Such a man is a vessel for new ideas; he can follow a spiritual movement. We see from this that the mother complex in itself is nothing abnormal—Dante was guided to Paradise by Beatrice as a mother figure! It means rather an inner structure which can be lived in either a positive or a negative way.

Notes

1. *The Confessions of St. Augustine,* trans. F. J. Sheed (New York: Sheed & Ward, 1943), pp. 55f.
2. C. G. Jung, *Psychological Types, CW* 6, par. 33.
3. Trans. Sheed, p. 179.
4. *The I Ching or Book of Changes,* trans. Cary F. Baynes from the Richard Wilhelm translation, 3d ed. (Princeton: Princeton University Press, 1967), p. 13 (Hexagram 2, *K'un*/The Receptive).
5. Cf. Marie-Louise von Franz, *The Passion of Perpetua* (Irving, Tex.: Spring Publications, 1979).
6. *De Genesi ad. litt.* 1.4. c. 3 and 8; *Patrologiae cursus completus* (*P.L.*), ed. Jacques Paul Migne, 34, col. 299.
7. Migne, *P.L.*, 210.
8. Jung, *Psychological Types,* pars. 20ff.

The Mothers of Saint Bernard and Saint Dominic

Translated by Emmanuel Xipolitas Kennedy and Vernon Brooks

When Aleth, the mother of Saint Bernard of Clairvaux, was pregnant she dreamed that she gave birth to a small white dog whose back was of a reddish color and which barked very loudly.

The mother of Saint Dominic, in identical circumstances, dreamed that she delivered a small dog carrying a shining torch in its mouth.

These dreams give one the impression that they have been invented, not only because they fit the circumstances of the dreamers so well but also because at the time dogs were a common allegorical image for saints and wise men. But even when a dream is invented it nevertheless often expresses the unconscious situation, as Jung has noted. The inventor of the dream would have found in these cases the suitable symbols for the two men, so that the "dream" nevertheless was inspired by the unconscious. It is as if the person who has a sudden idea is impregnated with an unconscious factor. However, I am of the opinion that these are authentic dreams.

Before discussing the various motifs in these two dreams, we need first to know something of the lives of the two saints.

The Life of Saint Bernard of Clairvaux (1092–1153)

Saint Bernard was born in Fontaine, near Dijon. His father, a knight named Tecelin, was killed on one of the crusades. His mother, Aleth, of an ancient family of noble lineage from Mon-Bar and famous for her piety, died when Bernard was young. Since the child had a weak constitution, she decided that he should become a monk and, despite some reluctance on his part, he joined the community (Cistercian) established by Robert of Molesmes in Citeaux in the year 1098. In 1115 he was appointed abbot of the abbey at Clairvaux, which later became the chief abbey of the Cistercians, and where he proved himself to be an effective teacher and saint who could heal through his touch. He was known far and wide for his miracles, and pilgrims streamed to him in great numbers.

Bernard was concerned with affairs of the world at large and participated in the most important theological debates of the time. At the Council of Troyes in 1128 he contributed to the council's approval of the new order of Knights Templar which had been founded for the fight against the Muhammadans and which was later infected with false doctrines and Arabic alchemy. Through them, however, secret Arabic alchemical teachings were introduced into Europe, where they were preserved until the sixteenth century. After the death of Pope Honorius II, Bernard successfully defended the claims of Innocent II against those of Anacletus II (the "Antichrist"). The pope traveled from place to place with the powerful abbot at his side, and thanks to Bernard the schism in the church was finally healed.

Saint Norbert had prophesized that the time of the Antichrist was near, for this had been revealed to him in a dream. Bernard did not believe it, however, and it was only after Anacletus (Petrus of Leone) came on the scene that he accepted Norbert's revelation.

The widespread extent of Bernard's influence is evident in the results of his battles with Abelard. Although he was morally strong, he was no match for the great scholar; a feeling type, he was unable to follow Abelard's subtle arguments—and yet his word was enough to effect a condemnation of the latter.

Bernard then directed his energy to fighting against the Albigenses in Languedoc. But the Second Crusade which he organized there failed to have any effect and reduced his influence in the church. This again frustrated his impulse to convert the Albigneses, and he attributed the steadfastness of "those dogs" in the face of death to the power of the Devil.[1]

By nature Bernard was neither a blind believer nor a persecutor and, apart from his fanaticism, had a noble character and a conciliatory, diplomatic manner. Broken by his harsh self-discipline and his never-ending labors, he died on 20 August 1153.

The Life of Saint Dominic (1170–1221)

Saint Dominic, founder of the Dominican order (Order of Preachers), was born in 1170 in Caleruega in Old Castile. He spent ten or twelve years in Palencia, where he studied mainly theology. He was ordained in the year 1195 as canon of the principal cathedral of Osma, his home diocese. In 1203 he accompanied his bishop on a royal embassy, in the name of the king of Castile, probably to France or Italy, where his remarkable diplomatic abilities were called forth.

Pope Innocent III commissioned him in 1205 to preach to the Albigenses in Languedoc, and for the next ten years that was his life's work (1205–1215).

The Albigenses of Languedoc were related to the Bogomils of Bulgaria, the Patarines of Lombardy, the Cathari, and so forth, whose teachings were Manichaean and Neoplatonic. The Bogomils, for instance, taught the existence of two deities, God and Satan, and that the material world was the realm of the Satanic master. For that reason they totally rejected the world and were great ascetics who renounced all earthly possessions. They even recommended suicide through voluntary starvation.

Dominic fought by the side of Simon de Montfort but did

not participate directly in the Crusade and was not an Inquisitor. His method was to talk and discuss with the Albigenses and to attempt to convince them with his sermons. Only when the results failed to correspond to his hopes did he resort to threats. In his final sermon in Languedoc he cried out bitterly, "For many years now I have admonished you with gentleness, through sermons, prayers, and tears. But where blessing did not help, a good beating may do the job!"

The Dominican order was organized by small groups of volunteers who joined Dominic during his mission to the Albigenses. In 1218 he received unqualified permission from Honorius III to found the order. It might seem that in his disappointment at having failed with the Albigenses, Dominic decided to go himself and preach to the Tatars on the Dnepr and the Volga. This, however, was not to be: he died, exhausted by hardship and his unceasing efforts as well as by the severity of his work-filled life, on 6 August 1221 in his monastery in Bologna.

Interpretation of the Dreams

Antiquity has provided us with a rich collection of dreams of the mothers of famous men. We may therefore consider the possibility that the dreams of those women foretold the fate and future importance of their child. We do not have many modern parallels, however. Jung was of the opinion that a woman should generally not be disturbed during pregnancy, for it is a time of brooding introversion. It was believed in older times that everything which impresses the mother during pregnancy has an influence on the soul of the unborn child. Therefore one can look at such a dream from two perspectives: as a prediction of the fate of the child, or as the disclosure of some problem in the soul of the mother herself.

Let us first examine these two dreams from the naive point of view, namely that they indicate the actual fate of the child.

Symbolism of the Dog

As a symbol, the dog has many aspects. In antiquity it was associated with the dark side of the moon, connected with the goddess Selene (moon), as well as with Artemis, the goddess of birth, who caused Actaeon to be torn to pieces by dogs because he saw her bathing. At night Hecate could be heard howling like a pack of dogs. Cerberus, the three-headed watchdog of Hades, was the child of Echidna, the half-snake, half-woman daughter of Gaia (the earth) and of Typhon. Their other children were the Chimera, Scylla, the Gorgon, the Nemean lion, and the eagle of Prometheus, as well as Othrus, dog of the monster Geryon, which Hercules killed. It was through this dog, her son Othrus, that Echidna gave birth to the sphinx.[2]

Sirius, the brightest star in the constellation Canis Major (the Great Dog), which rises and sets with the sun, is connected with the time of the most intense heat, the summer solstice. The dog appears in the Mithras mysteries as one of the animals which leap upon the dying bull; the death of Mithras as bull is the moment of the greatest fertility. At the time of the most intense heat, when the plague threatened (the Sirius period), dogs were sacrificed to Hecate. Isis, the Egyptian goddess, rides upon a dog. In antiquity there was a play on the words *kyon* and its genitive *kynos* ("dog") and *kyontis,* meaning "to be pregnant." Therefore *kyon,* the dog, was associated with pregnancy; the dog belonged to the Mother Goddess.

The Healing Motif of the Dog and Its Role as Psychopomp

Dogs were also an attribute of Aesculapius; they were his theriomorphic appearance. Because of their sense of smell, offerings were brought to them. In Egypt the jackal-headed Anubis assisted Isis in gathering the body parts of Osiris, all of which were found except the phallus which had been swallowed by the fish Oxymynchos. Dogs therefore also play the principal role in the death ritual; they are the priests of Anubis, whose office it is to make mummies of the corpses. In ancient Persia corpses were thrown to dogs for food; a dog was also brought to the bedside of a dying person in order to be fed by him so that the dogs would spare his body, just as Hercules gave Cerberus honey cakes on his journey to the underworld. There are often figures of small dogs on grave-stones, for dogs show the way to the Beyond. In Aztec mythology a small yellow dog guides people into the other world.

The dog motif was also found in the Gnostic systems. In his *Refutation of All Heresies,* Hippolytus speaks of the Dog Star and the constellation of Ursa Minor (the Little Bear) as actually being a dog and writes as follows:

> The Great Bear is the first creation; its way is that of a snail or of a wheel and it runs backward. The Little Bear is an imitation and the second creation, the narrow gateway to redemption, for it belongs to the constellation of the Dog. The *logos* is a dog; it protects the sheep from wolves; it creates the cosmos, that is, order. When the constellation of the Dog rises, all plants wither which have not yet put down deep roots; therefore the Dog Star is their judge. In the same way the dog, as *logos,* judges souls, if they have not yet found their deep roots.[3]

A Gnostic text refers to a blue dog-shaped woman who is chased by an ithyphallic man; she is therefore the companion of the moon in a dark *coniunctio* (union).[4] The *logos*-form of the dog is also emphasized in Christian symbolism, that is, it is an image of Christ, gentle toward those who accept him, dangerous for his opponents. Saint Gregory referred to pious and learned men as dogs. Saint Paul was compared to an Indian dog, which lives half in the earth, half in water.

In alchemical symbolism the dog indicates the beginning of transformation; it is a symbol of the *prima materia.* Thus Ventura, citing Arnaldus, directs the adept: "Break the small female dog into pieces (*frange caniculam*)," indicating that the bitch, like the male dog, is a symbol of the *prima materia,* which must be dissolved in order to be transformed. A quota-tion of Hermes in Khalid says that one must "take a Coetanean dog and an Armenian bitch, mate them, and they will bear you a son in the likeness of a dog of a celestial hue" and that "this dog will guard your friend and he will guard you from your enemy and he will help you wherever you may be, always being with you, in this world and in the next."[5]

The Realistic Aspect of the Dog-Image

Cuvier said once, "The dog is one of man's greatest conquests." It is used in hunting and as a guardian. It is at once pure nature and yet the most related of all the animals to man; psychologically it represents mankind's ideal contact with his instincts. It is known in folklore because of its good nose, and it is said that it foresees the future. Dogs know when people die, and sometimes they starve by the grave of their master. They are so much a mirror of man that they really represent his *alter ego*. There are numerous examples of this close association; one need only mention Frederick the Great and his "Bichette."

Now let us apply the symbolism of the dog to the two dreams.

The dog has lost his independence and become dependent on human beings. Both Saint Bernard and Saint Dominic were also servants of a master: Christ. This is the motif of *katochē*.[6] They are the prisoners of a special fate; every impulse to live their own life is controlled; they are really the dogs of Christ,[7] serving him in this world and as dogs leading to hope of the other world. They are also responsible for keeping the flock together, since heretics are the wolves or "the little foxes, that spoil the vines."[8]

These particular "dogs," however, have a negative aspect as well, for they served only one point of view; they did not deal with the problem of their time. Bernard was incapable of engaging in discussion with Abelard, he only "barked" at him! And Dominic "barked" at the Albigenses. We must not overlook the fact that this was the beginning of the Inquisition, which attempted to eliminate, through sheer power, every heretical movement. As a result, however, the religious confrontation became increasingly fanatic. Such a solution of the conflict is no solution; but at that time man was not yet capable of dealing with the problem in an individual, humane manner.

Both of these men were feeling types, full of loyalty to their feeling. Bernard could heal through touching; this reminds us of the motif of the dog of Aesculapius, and also of Anubis. In a certain sense Bernard also healed the split in the church. When such a man follows an inner course, which does not seem to be his consciously acquired view of the times, it presumably means that his instinctive convictions come from the mother; she has transplanted into her son her emotional opinions, as in Augustine's case; but then the son is simply carried by an unchecked impulse; he detours around the inner conflict of religious doubt and consequently engages in conflict with the *outer world*. Abelard tried to reconcile Aristotelianism with the theological thinking of his time, to unite realism and nominalism in his conceptualism; he tried to think in paradoxes and at the same time to endure the conflict in real life. Neither of our saints was troubled by inner temptations and doubt; for them the wolves and foxes were outside, and they barked at them. They were carried unconsciously by instinct. With them the Christian tradition had become an instinctive attitude, through which they were always supported from beneath. But this also brings about a certain inertia toward probing into things and working through them in oneself.

As mentioned above, we must also consider the negative aspects of the dog: as dark Mother Hecate, as death and as the bringer of madness. If we examine this aspect with regard to both of these men, we see that their pious, zealous attitude, minus any humaneness, had very negative results at that time. The dog "carrying a shining torch in its mouth" was interpreted at the time as "bringing light into the world." This is true, on the one hand, for the Dominican order was the birthplace of Thomistic philosophy and of the scholastic spirit in the Roman Catholic church. Their intention was not to take refuge in the Inquisition, but to use better arguments, and in this way ecclesiastical philosophy produced a new form of European thinking which was of the greatest importance. Naturally one gets infected by what one fights, and that is why Aristotelianism and a good part of antique magic (i.e., natural science) stole into this new philosophical teaching—

even seventeen *sententiae* of Thomas Aquinas were condemned! As a result of this scholastic movement, the intellectual side of the dogma was developed; however, the naive feeling experience of early Christianity was partly lost and was compensated by the birth of mystic movements (Meister Eckhart, Richard, Hugh, and Adam of Saint Victor, etc.).

The stiffening against heretical movements also caused a certain inflexibility in the dogmatic attitude and led gradually to the later unfortunate schism in the Church. We should therefore interpret the torch motif not only as illumination but also as a sign of a future conflagration: it will set the world on fire. Fire is in itself an accumulation of energy, of affects and emotions, which literally cause destruction but also bring illumination. It is the carrier of a new enlightenment, without which we would never be able to reach a higher consciousness. This torch brought with it a difficult conflict, but it was also the midwife for a new European spirit in which we still live to some extent today. In the dream the unconscious brings the motif without commentary, as a snapshot, so to speak, of the momentary situation.

If we compare the two dream dogs with each other, we see that Bernard's dog was quite an ordinary one, whereas that of Dominic, with the torch in its mouth, was not. Primitives would call the latter a "doctor-dog," the hidden carrier of a spirit. This gives the dog a supernatural background: it is a kind of spirit in veiled form. We must now ask ourselves how we are to interpret this motif of the dog as an animal that stands behind man and supports him. It points to a possibility, a tendency to raise its meaning up into consciousness, and indicates that there is, at the same time, an incompatibility in consciousness; due to certain prejudices we do not allow the contents to pass over the conscious human threshold.

Bernard's dog represents another motif; although it is a dog, it is white and red. These two colors belong to the color stages of the alchemical process; first comes the *nigredo* (blackening), sometimes followed by the peacock's-tail or green color; then the *albedo* (whitening), afterward the *rubedo* (reddening) and with it, as fourth stage, the yellow or golden color.

The *nigredo* indicates a condition of depression and sadness, a condition of being driven by instinctive impulses, passions (the appearance of wild animals), emotions, etc. Shadow and animus or anima appear in this stage in a destructive form. For this reason the *albedo* is produced through washing and cleaning. The *albedo* represents a condition of illumination; new connections become clear, one becomes detached and more objective in view of one's inner impulses; one stands above one's emotions. This is the time when the "white snow is suddenly seen to fly."[9] But in this stage one is also cut off from life, too lonely, too separate, too passive. Then comes the *rubedo,* or reddening; life returns, it is no longer ruled by the ego, but by the Self, there is a relation between the two once again, but in an impersonal way.

The alchemical symbolism is not in opposition to the Christian view of the times, it supplements it, so to speak, it strives to add the missing black stages and thereby to complete Christianity in its relation to reality and to the genuine human being. Around the year A.D. 1000 there was a crisis in Christianity, and these two saints, as well as alchemy, tried in their respective ways to heal it; the saints barked at the wolves, whereas the goal of alchemy was to promote man's increasing consciousness.

Let us now interpret the dream from the point of view of the mother. In fairy tales we often encounter the motif of the evil stepmother or mother-in-law who slanders the young mother and announces to her son that his wife has given birth to dogs, which indicates sodomy. There are women who have similar fantasies before childbirth.

What does the dream mean psychologically? The intention of the unconscious is to help the woman realize something in order that the son is freed to follow his own fate. Aleth was concerned about this motif and afraid that she would not bear a normal child. She was French, from a good family, and was confronted with a very difficult problem: her husband was constantly away from home; she could not live her instincts without sinning. In ancient Greece "dog" was a vulgar word for the penis and represented ordinary sexuality; thus the so-called "dog philosophers," the Cynic school, for instance, practiced intercouse in public in order to show their contempt for all conventions. In her spiritual life Aleth was equally frustrated, since a woman needs human community as well as Eros in order to develop properly. If she cannot live her Eros in reality, then the unconscious becomes overloaded; if the instinct suffers, she can get a spirit-dog as a lover for herself. With such women the unconscious is excessively constellated, and this increases the fantasies they have about their sons. When a woman stays alone, she often falls into the animus. The Arabs say of a woman who leads a lonely life that a djinn has captured her in the desert!

Although many women have perhaps had similar dreams, they are not always lived out in the same way. These dreams reveal only a particular pattern, and on what level this pattern is lived depends on the human peculiarity of mother and son. Bernard and Dominic lived the pattern of a mother complex, but in a high and admirable form. In such cases the goal of analysis is to discover how such a powerful mother complex, which cannot be changed, can be lived. Such factors are too deep to be eliminated. We are dealing with a basic archetypal pattern; it cannot be arrested, it can only be lived in a human and acceptably adequate way, compatible with the personal values of the man whose soul it contains. With the saints it results in a sacrifice of personal values, and the church is right to canonize them. Another man would perhaps live the life of a real dog on an ordinary level. When a mother suppresses her instinctual life, then the son will probably live it out to an excessive extent. But he can only do this if he manages to break away. More often, however, he will live the wishes of his mother *not* to come *at all* into contact with the world.

These two men never tried to break out; they lived within their limitations, they took the sacrifice of their personal lives upon themselves—but they projected the dark onto their enemies.

Notes

1. Sermo 66, concerning the Song of Songs 2:15.
2. On the symbolism of the dog, cf. Jung, *Symbols of Transformation, CW* 5, par. 577.
3. *Elenchos* 4. 47. 10ff. Translated by the author.
4. Ibid., 5. 20.6.
5. See also the *Rosarium* and the quotation in Jung, *The Practice of Psychotherapy*, par. 458.
6. Cf. von Franz, *The Passion of Perpetua* (Irving, Tex.: Spring Publications, 1979), p. 44.
7. In a play on words the Dominicans called themselves *Domini canes,* "dogs of the Lord."
8. Song of Songs, 2:15.
9. R. Wilhelm and C. G. Jung, *The Secret of the Golden Flower,* (New York: Harcourt, Brace & World, 1962), p. 53.

The
Dream of
Descartes

Translated by Andrea Dykes and Elizabeth Welsh

Introduction

The so-called "great dream" of young René Descartes has always attracted great interest, for Descartes himself considered it of first importance. He thought it worthy of publication and tried to interpret its symbolism. Indisputably this dream played a decisive role in Descartes's development, but unfortunately we have only an incomplete version of its content, related by the Abbé Adrien Baillet.[1]

The dream has not been investigated much from the standpoint of depth psychology. But Sigmund Freud once said to Maxim Leroy that it was a dream "from above," i.e., from a layer of the psyche very close to consciousness. Therefore, most of its content could have been produced consciously.[2] Also, two articles in the *International Journal of Psycho-Analysis* for 1939 and 1947 explain the dream from the Freudian point of view.[3] I shall discuss these articles later, in the course of my own interpretation. An excellent study by J. Rittmeister, "Die

Reprinted from *Timeless Documents of the Soul,* ed. Helmuth Jacobsohn (Evanston, Ill.: Northwestern University Press, 1968), 57–137, by permission of Northwestern University Press.

mystische Krise des jungen Descartes," written earlier but published later than this paper, interprets the dream in agreement with my own version in many respects. Rittmeister died in Germany in 1943. His paper was posthumously published by A. Storch,[4] who also wrote a short comparison of our interpretations.

Although the articles investigating Descartes's dream have uncovered much information about his personal problems, we believe that the dream, in symbolic form, also throws considerable light on the spiritual situation at the beginning of the seventeenth century, revealing aspects that still interest us today.[5] To use Jung's term, this is an archetypal dream. It contains a suprapersonal message. The dream's basic symbols—the storm, the round fruit, the sparks of fire, and the "magic trickery"—are all *archetypal images* with a collective meaning showing that the events which took place in Descartes's unconscious and pushed their way into the light of his mind were deeply enmeshed in the general religious and scientific problems of his time. Because the personal aspect is also of great importance, we must consider it first.[6]

Descartes's Life

René Descartes was born at La Haye (Touraine) on 31 March 1596, the third living child of Joachim des Cartes,[7] a councilor in the *parlement* of Rennes. His mother, Jeanne Brochard, died a year later in giving birth to a fifth child, who did not survive.[8] His father married a second time. Descartes tells us that he inherited his mother's pale countenance and incessant cough.[9] At the age of eight he was sent to the Royal Jesuit college of La Flèche in Anjou. There Father Etienne Charlet and Father Dinet considerately permitted him to take good care of his delicate health. Since he had a room to himself, he used to lie in bed meditating—a habit which clung to him throughout his life—and his schoolfellows dubbed him "*le chambriste.*"[10] His father had little use for the delicate boy always buried in his books or lost in his thoughts.[11] But Descartes got along well with his sister, later Madame de

Crévy, and her son. At sixteen he left La Flèche to live in Paris. Here he associated with his friends, Mydorge and others (possibly Mersenne). With them he devoted himself to mathematics, music, and philosophy—chiefly the writings of skeptics like Montaigne and Charron. He led the life of a typical *gentilhomme*, fencing, riding, playing *jeu de paume*, playing music; women, however, he politely avoided.[12] In Paris, too, he used to spend most of the morning in bed, withdrawing more and more into complete seclusion. He continued these habits when taking part in the Netherlands campaign of Maurice of Nassau (who was Protestant, but allied to France) against the Spaniards.[13]

The protracted siege of Breda was a period of leisure for Descartes, which he employed in indulging his philosophical bent. He also became acquainted with the Dordrecht physicist and doctor Isaak Beeckmann, with whom he chiefly discussed the application of mathematics to physics, and vice versa.[14]

In 1619 he attended the coronation of Ferdinand II of Austria in Frankfurt and stayed quartered in the neighborhood of Ulm, where he spent the whole winter, spiritually incubating in a warm room (*"dans un poêle"*) in the house of a German middle-class family. There Descartes experienced his famous "enlightenment," his great mathematical discovery, and the ensuing dream, which we are about to discuss. He was then twenty-three years of age. All we really know further about this important phase of his life is that he was probably already in touch with the Rosicrucian Johannes Faulhaber[15] and was much impressed by the movement.[16] Whether he actually joined the society is uncertain and indeed unlikely.[17] In his *Discours de la méthode* he says he owned to having read the alchemists and magicians enough not to be taken in by them.[18] He was undoubtedly acquainted with Agrippa of Nettesheim's works and Raimundus Lullus's *Ars Magna*,[19] as well as Athanasius Kircher's *De Magnete*[20] and Joannes Baptista's *Magia Naturalis*.

Previously, at La Flèche, he had become acquainted with the works of Galileo, who was only later condemned by the Church. In particular, Lullus and the question of astrology haunted him (*hanté*) for a long time.[21] He had probably read the alchemical treatise *Physika kai mystika* of Pseudo-Democritus and had named a work of his own *Democritica,* after it.[22] After countless fruitless wanderings and a relatively passive part in the Battle of the White Mountain near Prague, against the "Winter King," Friedrich von der Pfalz, Descartes returned to Paris. In 1623 he went on a pilgrimage to the Madonna of Loretto near Venice,[23] in fulfillment of a vow which he had made on the occasion of his dream. He then took part in certain Church festivals being celebrated in Rome.

The conflict between the freethinkers (such as Vanini) and the Church made life in France impossible for him; however, when called upon by the Jesuit Cardinal de Berulle to oppose the freethinker Chandoux in a debate, he triumphed over his opponent.[24]

Descartes therefore went to live in Holland, where foreign trade and colonial expansion were at their height; this was the time of Rembrandt and Frans Hals.[25] He changed his lodgings no less than twenty-four times and kept his address as secret as possible. Because he greatly loved nature, he sought places to live in the country. His residence was usually divided into two parts: a *salon de réception* and, behind it, a secret laboratory where he dissected animals (even going so far as to vivisect rabbits),[26] ground and polished telescope lenses, and undertook other kinds of scientific work.[27] During this period he was working on *Le Monde,* a kind of encyclopedia of all the natural sciences. But after Galileo's condemnation he did not dare to publish it,[28] because in it he defended a Galilean theory which was related to some of his own.[29] He distributed its content throughout his other works, with the result that parts of it did not come out until after his death. At this time his first discussions with his orthodox philosophical opponents took place, the latter accusing him of undermining religion. He sought and found support from his old master, Father Dinet of La Flèche, and diplomatic and political protection through the French embassy. Indeed, he was most unwilling to face philosophical battles and avoided them in a peaceable and diplomatic spirit.[30] At this time his *Principia* was published, as well as his correspondence with Elisabeth von der Pfalz on the relation of body and mind. This latter gave rise to his treatise *Les Passions de l'âme.*[31]

At this stage of his life, Descartes entered into a liaison with a Dutch maidservant, Helena Jans, which resulted in the birth of a daughter, Francine. But the little girl died when she was about five years old,[32] and we hear nothing more of the mother. Descartes speaks of this episode as a "dangerous engagement from which God had rescued him" ("dangereux engagement dont Dieu l'a retiré") and emphasizes later "that God, by a continuation of His same grace, had preserved him up to then from backsliding" ("que Dieu par une continuation de Sa même grâce, l'avait préservé jusque-là de la récidive"). In a letter he admits to having had in his youth a passing fancy for a girl with a slight squint. The same remarkably cold feeling—or perhaps fear of accepting his feeling—is shown in the expression he uses when speaking of the almost simultaneous death of his sister and father, namely, that he experienced a considerable "désplaisir."[33]

In his portraits Descartes appears to us extremely skeptical, with altogether lusterless, mistrustful, and inward-looking eyes. He was small, delicately built, dressed mostly in black, and painfully neat. He wore his hair falling over his forehead like a black curtain reaching almost to his eyes.

In 1649, through his friend Pierre Chanut, French ambassador to Sweden, Descartes was appointed tutor in philosophy to Queen Christina of Sweden,[34] a girl just twenty years old. The poor *chambriste* had to give his lessons in the very early hours of the morning.[35] Moreover, his young pupil, whose Spartan habits and unbounded energy seem to have been the result of a fierce animus-possession, forced on him the reorganization of the academic system in Sweden. However, while devotedly nursing Chanut, who was suffering from inflammation of the lungs, Descartes himself contracted the disease and died on 11 February 1650, in his fifty-fourth year.

The events immediately preceding the dream are vague, but we do know definitely that the young Descartes dreamed it in his *poêle* in Ulm in the first year of the catastrophic Thirty Years' War. This dream made such a deep impression on him that he published it in a special paper, *Olympica*,[36] thus intimating that he felt it had "come from above"—although evidently not from the God of Christianity. Leibniz made fun of the "chimerical" nature of this work.[37] The content of the original work, which was lost, is related in Adrien Baillet's *La Vie de M. Descartes*.[38]

The Dream

Descartes begins his account of the dream with the following words: "On the 10th of November, 1619, when I was filled with enthusiasm and discovered the foundations of the marvelous science."[39] In the margin we read: "On November 11th, 1620, I began to understand the fundamentals of the marvelous discovery."[40] It is evidently a case of inspiration or unconscious enlightenment; not until a year had passed did he begin to understand it consciously and to make use of it.[41] At the time of the dream he was in a state of extreme exhaustion, the result of having striven passionately to free his mind from all prejudice so that he could experience his mind in an absolutely pure state (*"intellectus purus"*) and by this means discover the truth—the sole aim of his life.[42] As he tells us in *Discours de la méthode*,[43] he turned his attention entirely within:

> After I had spent some years thus studying in the book of the world and in trying to acquire some experience, I one day made the resolution to study *within myself also,* and to use all the powers of my mind for the choosing of the paths that I ought to follow; in the which I succeeded far better, so it seems to me, than if I had never left my country or my books.[44]

It is probably no chance event that Descartes's great dream occurred during his German "exile," because, for the French, Germany often represents the "landscape of the soul," upon which they project their unconscious—their shadow and romantic side—as well as their lack of moderation, speculative thinking, and so forth. Descartes describes his new experiment as a wandering in the dark:[45] "But like a man who walks alone in the dark, I resolved to go so slowly, and to use so much circumspection in all things that, even if I possessed very little, I at least took good care not to fall."[46] Thus he arrived quite close to the threshold of the unconscious and even had a premonition that he would have a meaningful dream that night.[47] He says, in fact, that the same spirit (*"le génie"*) which inspired him with enthusiasm had already predicted the dream when he went to bed and that the human mind had no part in this dream.[48] G. Cohen, who claims Descartes for the Rosicrucians, also calls special attention to the following significant rhythm in his life: on 10 November 1618, the meeting with Isaak Beeckmann, his spiritual awakener, as Descartes calls him; on 10 November 1619, the great dream; and on 11 November 1620, the discovery of the *"scientia mirabilis,"* or the possibilities of its application.[49]

It is impossible to identify with any degree of certainty the "marvelous discovery" which, as he says, he made on the evening preceding the dream.[50] It might consist, first, in his discovery that the four subjects of the quadrivium—mathematics, geometry, arithmetic, and astronomy—can, together with music,[51] all be reduced to one *"mathématique universelle,"* whose basic principles are the seriality of numbers and their proportionate relations;[52] second, that algebra can be expressed by the letters of the alphabet, and the square and cubic numbers, etc., by small superscript numbers instead of by the so-called Cossic signs; and third, that quantities can be expressed by lines and vice versa, whereby geometry, algebra, and mathematics are fused and become *one* scientific discipline: analytical geometry.[53]

G. Milhaud has shown, however, that the "discovery" was in all likelihood first worked out *after* the dream,[54] so I would surmise that at this time Descartes probably perceived these connections only intuitively and then later worked them out in the aforementioned specific formulations.

I should like to illustrate this idea by Poincaré's explanation of the genesis of mathematical discoveries, about which he has written a psychological study of outstanding interest.[55] Poincaré begins with the fact that not all gifted thinkers are mathematically gifted and comes to the conclusion that "A mathematical *proof* is not a simple following-on of syllogisms, but it is a series of syllogisms *that are brought into a specific order,* and the order in which the individual elements here appear is far more important than these elements themselves."[56] According to Poincaré, mathematical talent is an intuitive feeling for mathematical order,[57] and mathematical discovery occurs through preconscious selection from the abundance of given possibilities of combinations. Poincaré then relates how he himself made just such a discovery:

> For two weeks I had been exerting myself to prove that there existed no functions of the kind that I have subsequently named Fuchsian functions. At that time I was very inexperienced; every day I sat at my writing-table for one or two hours, experimenting with a great number of combinations without achieving any result. One evening, contrary to my habit, I drank some black coffee and was unable to sleep. A lot of thoughts crowded in. I felt how they collided with one another, until finally two of them clung together and formed a stable combination. By morning I had proved the existence of a class of Fuchsian functions, those very ones that are deducible from the hypergeometric series. I only needed to revise the result, which was accomplished in a few hours.[58]

Poincaré then tells of a further similar discovery that, in the form of a sudden thought, appeared before his eyes with absolute certainty as he was out walking one day. Further on he says:

> The irruption of this sudden enlightenment is very surprising; in it we see a sure sign of prior long-continued unconscious work; the importance of such unconscious work for mathematical discovery is incontestable. . . . When one is working on a difficult problem, it often happens that at the start of the work one makes no progress. One then allows oneself a shorter or longer break for rest and thereafter sits down again at one's desk. During the first half-hour one again finds nothing, and then suddenly the decisive idea presents itself. . . . Probably unconscious work went on during the rest period, and the result of this labor is later revealed to the mathematician. . . . But such

a revelation does not only occur during a walk or a journey. It also asserts itself during a period of conscious work, but in this case it is independent of that work, and the latter acts at most as a catalyst; it is similar to the stimulus that incited the result—gained during the time of rest, but that had remained unconscious—to take on conscious form. . . .[59]

Indeed, the often fruitless exertions concerning the problem bring, as it were, the activities of the unconscious into play, and its results appear in consciousness as inspirations.

The specially privileged unconscious manifestations which are capable of appearing in consciousness are those that, either directly or indirectly, influence our sensibility most profoundly. It will be noticed with amazement that here, on this occasion of mathematical argument which appears to be dependent solely on the intelligence, the feelings have to be brought into consideration. It becomes intelligible, however, if one pictures to oneself the feeling for mathematical beauty. The feeling for the harmony of numbers and forms, for geometrical elegance . . . offers satisfaction to our aesthetic needs and at the same time provides help for our mind, which it sustains and guides. Insofar as it unfolds a well-ordered whole before our eyes, it permits us to anticipate a mathematical law.[60]

I think that these observations of Poincaré's can give us an idea of what happened to Descartes on the eve of his dream. He must have experienced a similar mathematical "enlightenment" or intuitive vision of certain combinations or ordered patterns and may possibly even have drawn the (somewhat premature) conclusion that in this "enlightenment" he had discovered either a kind of universal science or its laws. A passionate war is still being waged today between members of the so-called "formalistic" school of mathematics, who believe that mathematics is based on conscious lemmata (as, for instance, Bertrand Russell and G. Frege, among others), and the intuitives, who concede that mathematical discoveries can originate from an intuitive vision of mathematical order. In his *The Psychology of Invention in the Mathematical Field*,[61] Jacques Hadamard has shown that mathematical discoveries are in all probability often ruled by preconscious psychic processes. I believe that at this period of his life Descartes had a mathematical intuition, which he later tried to work out through rational thinking.

According to Sirven,[62] Descartes had, even at that time, already intuitively perceived his whole *"méthode,"* that is, his way of thinking, and the mathematical discoveries were the first of its fruits. Sirven believes, however, that the *"méthode"* was based on the still generally held idea of the unity of all the sciences (*"l'unité des sciences"*). Its first yield is the idea of a *"mathématique universelle."* As E. Gilson emphasizes,[63] for Descartes it is a case of "tout ce qui est susceptible de connaissance vraie . . . est par définition susceptible de connaissance mathématique. L'idée de l'unité du corps des sciences[64] . . . est donc inséparable, chronologiquement et logiquement, de l'extension de la méthode mathématique à la totalité du domaine de la connaissance."[65] This belief in unity was easy for Descartes, who considered mathematical knowledge to be "absolute truths."[66]

This conviction has since collapsed, and the reality basis of mathematical thinking has become a matter of passionate discussion. Mathematicians today are aware, as Professor F. Gonseth explains,[67] that mathematical thinking takes place in a "field of consciousness" between two complementary poles of reality: one called "outer" and one called "inner," both of which transcend consciousness.[68] Descartes saw these two realms as coincident in their orderedness and did not concern himself with their consciousness-transcending, "transmathematical" nature.[69] He believed, rather, that he was able to grasp their mystery by mathematics alone. Probably what he really had in his mind was the immanent orderedness of the thought processes that had been released[70] by the archetypes (his "numbers" and *"veritates innatae"*) and, with them, *the idea of an "absolute knowledge."*[71] He clearly thought that he could formulate this best through the basic concepts of mathematics or else, more generally, through a universal scientific method and symbolic language.[72] I think this was the reason Raimundus Lullus's *Ars Magna* "pursued" him for so long a period, since it represents a similar effort to "apprehend" an "absolute truth" through the means of mathematical symbolism. Lullus's work was also based on an unconscious inspiration[73] and hence earned him the title of *doctor illuminatus*. It consisted in a correlation of certain ancient mnemotechnical arts whereby the orator hoped to commit his speech to memory without effort. Metrodorus of Skepsis had invented an art by which he associated the parts of any oration he was to deliver with the "magic circle" of the zodiacal houses. This idea, which at first sight seems so absurd, is really not so when we realize that through the present-day depth psychology of Jung it has been discovered that the central ordering of preconscious psychic processes is due to a psychic regulatory center which Jung has designated "the Self" and which is known to manifest itself in mandala form.[74] The horoscope and Lullus's patterns of thought are structures of this kind.[75] In these mnemotechnical mandalas we consequently see a first prescientific idea that the Self can be the ultimate "regulating factor" of our thought processes and memory structures. These mnemotechnical mandalas, which were also meant to serve for the ordering and concentration of the soul, flourished during the Renaissance (Marsilio Ficino and Pico della Mirandola) and were even thought to have a magical regenerating power on the Universe (Giordano Bruno).[76] They were supposed to represent an image of a mysterious all-comprehending order of the Cosmos in the soul of man. As Paolo Rossi has most convincingly demonstrated, these traditions exerted a profound influence on the young Descartes. With this idea—that by constructing a mandala one can find a common structural model of the universe *and* of the human mind—was connected the hope that it would be possible to discover a kind of "ideas-computer"—a generally valid logical system by which all essential knowledge could be collected.[77] It appears extremely probable that Descartes was influenced by ideas such as these and that intuitively he looked to something like a universal order of being (presumably in mandala form) and was emotionally overwhelmed by the thought that he had had a glimpse into the central mystery of all being. It is therefore natural to suppose that his vision was a mandala because the Cartesian system of coordinates that resulted from these intuitions is also a mandala. G. Milhaud considers that he had found "things of a higher order, things divine or heavenly" ("des choses d'en haut, des choses divines ou célestes") and had therefore christened his treatise *Olympica*,[78] just as, in his dream, he had interpreted the storm as the "mind" and the lightning as the "spirit of truth."[79] Milhaud is therefore inclined to think that Descartes had found a *universal language of symbolic interpretation,* something that reaches out even beyond pure mathematics. At all events, it seems probable that Descartes was touched by some archetypal ordered images of the unconscious and sought to comprehend them intellectually. Numbers *are* archetypal representations, which seem to be based on archetypal patterns that actually *do* unite the worlds of psyche and matter in a still unexplained way. Also, the Rosicrucian Johannes Faulhaber, with whom Descartes was probably in communication at the time, had in 1619 brought out a book, *Numerus figuratus sive Arithmetica arte mirabili*[80] *inaudita nova constans,* on the symbolism of numbers.[81] At that time Descartes, too, was planning to write a book entitled "Trésor mathématique de Polybe le Cosmopolite." Perhaps he was seeking to set up universally derived principles of thinking out of the order of natural integers such as, for instance, result from the proportional relations of numbers.[82] He certainly was looking for a mathematical-symbolic universal science and believed that he had had a presentiment of its rudiments[83] and its "language."

Here is Adrien Baillet's rendering of Descartes's account of the dream:[84]

Descartes tells us that when he lay down to sleep on 10 November 1619, he was still filled with enthusiasm and was completely absorbed by the thought of having that day discovered the foundations of a "marvelous science." During the night he had three consecutive dreams, which he thought could only have been inspired by a higher power. Having fallen asleep, he imagined he saw *ghosts* and was terrified by these appearances. He thought he walked through the streets, and he was so horrified by the visions that he had to bend over on his left side[85] in order to reach his objective, for he felt a great weakness in his right side and was unable to hold himself up. Ashamed at having to walk in this fashion, he made a great effort to straighten himself, but *he was struck by a violent wind.* The wind seized him like a *whirlwind* and made him spin round three or four times on his left foot. It was not this, however, which frightened him most. He found it was so difficult to advance that he was afraid of falling at every step, until, perceiving [the gates to] a college standing open on his path, he entered, *to seek refuge* and help in his affliction. He endeavored to reach the *college chapel,* where his first thought was to pray; but, *realizing that he had passed by an acquaintance without greeting him,* he wished, out of politeness, to turn back. [Attempting to do so, however,] *he was thrown back with violence by the wind, which was blowing toward the church.* At the same instant he perceived *another man in the college courtyard,* who called Descartes politely by his name and informed him that, if he were seeking Mr. N., he had something for him. Descartes had the impression *that this [object] must be a melon which had been brought from some exotic land.* Great was his astonishment when he noticed that the people who had gathered around the man, to chat with one another, were able to stand upright and firm on their feet, whereas, on the same spot, he himself had to walk crookedly and unsteadily, even though the wind, which had several times threatened to throw him over, had abated considerably.

At this point he awoke, feeling a definite pain. *He feared it was the effect of evil spirits, bent on leading him astray.* He immediately turned over onto his right side, for it was on his left side that he had fallen asleep and had the dream. He prayed to God to protect him from the evil consequences of his dream and to preserve him from all the misfortunes which might threaten him as a punishment for his sins. He recognized that his sins were grievous enough to call down all the wrath of heaven on his head, although up till then, in the eyes of men, he had led a fairly irreproachable life. *He lay awake about two hours, pondering the problem of good and evil in this world,* and then fell asleep.

Another dream followed immediately. *He thought he heard a shrill and violent report,* which he took to be a thunderclap [*coup de foudre*]. He was so terrified that he awoke at once.

On opening his eyes, he became aware of a multitude of *fiery sparks* scattered throughout the room. This had often happened to him before, and it was not unusual for him to wake up in the middle of the night to find that his sight was clear enough for him to perceive the objects nearest to him. This time, however, he determined to resort to explanations borrowed from philosophy and, opening and shutting his eyes alternately and observing the nature of the objects which met his sight, he drew favorable conclusions, which appeared convincing to his mind. Thus his fear vanished, and with a quiet mind he again fell asleep.

Soon afterward he had a third dream, which was not so terrible as the previous two.

In this last dream he found a book on his table, not knowing who had laid it there. He opened it and was delighted to see that it was a *dictionary,* hoping that it might be very *useful* to him. The next instant *another book* appeared, just as new to him as the first and its origin equally unknown. He found that it was a collection of poems by different authors, entitled *Corpus Poetarum,* etc. (in the margin: "Divided into five books, printed in Lyon and Geneva, etc.").[86] He was curious to find out what it contained, and on opening the book his eye fell on the line "Quod vitae sectabor iter?" At the same time *he saw a man whom he did not know,* who showed him a poem beginning with the words "Est et non," and extolled its excellence. Descartes told him that he knew the poem, which was among the idylls of Ausonius and was included in the big collection of poems which lay on his table. He wanted to show it to the man and began turning over the leaves of the book, boasting that he knew the order and arrangement perfectly. As he was looking for the place, the man asked him where he had got the book. Descartes answered that he could not tell him how he had got it but that, a second before, *he had had another book in his hands, which had just disappeared,* without his knowing who had brought it or who had taken it away again. He had hardly finished speaking when the book reappeared at the other end of the table. He discovered, however, that the dictionary was no longer complete,[87] though earlier it had appeared to be so. Meanwhile, he found the poems of Ausonius in the anthology of poets, which he was running through; but, being unable to find the poem beginning "Est et non," he told the man that he knew an even more beautiful poem by the same author, beginning "Quod vitae sectabor iter?" The man begged to let him see it, and Descartes was diligently searching for it when he came upon *a number of small portraits—copperplate engravings*—which made him exclaim at the beauty of the book; but it was not the same edition as the one he knew.

At this point both the man and the books disappeared and faded from his mind's eye, but he did not awaken. The remarkable thing is that, being in doubt as to whether this experience was a dream or a vision, he not only decided, while still sleeping, that it was a dream, but he also interpreted it before waking. He concluded that *the dictionary signified the connection between all the sciences* and that the collection of poets entitled *Corpus Poetarum* pointed particularly and clearly to *the intimate union of philosophy with wisdom.* For he thought that one should not be surprised to discover that the poets, even those whose work seems to be only a foolish pastime, produce much deeper, more sensible, and better expressed thoughts than are to be found in the writings of the philosophers. *He attributed this wonder to the divine quality of enthusiasm and the power of imagination,* which enable the *seed of wisdom (existing in the minds of all men as do sparks of fire in flint)*[88] to sprout with much greater ease and even brilliance than the "reason" of the philosophers. Continuing to interpret the dream in his sleep, Descartes concluded that the poem on "what sort of life one should choose," beginning "Quod vitae sectabor iter," pointed to the sound advice of a wise person or even to Moral Theology. Still uncertain whether he was dreaming or meditating, he awoke peacefully and with open eyes continued to interpret his dream in the same spirit. The poets represented in the collection of poems he interpreted as the revelation and enthusiasm that had been accorded him. The poem "Est et non"—which is the "Yes and No" of Pythagoras—he understood as the truth and error of all human knowledge and profane science. When he saw that all these things were so satisfactorily turning out according to his desire, he dared to believe that it was the *spirit of truth* that wished, through this dream, to reveal to him the treasures of all the sciences. There now remained nothing to be explained save the small copperplate portraits that he had found in the second book. These he no longer sought to elucidate after receiving a visit from an Italian painter on the following day.

Interpretation of the First Dream

The exposition of the dream consists in the rather hazy statement that Descartes was frightened by the presence of "a number of ghosts" and thought he was walking through streets toward an (unknown) goal. His fear caused him to bend over on his left side (*"se renverser"*), since he felt a great weakness on the right.

The ghostly apparitions might well be connected with his experience of the previous day,[89] for they are the primordial form of the "spirit," an embodiment, in other words, of the autonomous image-creating activity of the unconscious,[90] which primitive man has always experienced as ghosts or spirits.[91]

While this is the form in which the mind actually confronts primitive man, "with increasing development it enters the realm of human consciousness and becomes a function under man's control; whereby its original autonomous character is apparently lost."[92] Man, however, should never forget

> what he draws into his sphere and with what he fills his consciousness. For he has not created the mind, it is the mind which enables him to create; it gives him the impulse, the sudden flash of insight, endurance, enthusiasm, and inspiration. But it so penetrates the human being that man is sorely tempted to believe that he himself is the creator of the spirit and that he owns it. In reality, however, it is the primordial phenomenon of the mind that takes possession of man, and in exactly the same way as that in which the physical world appears to be the willing tool of his purpose but in reality tears man's freedom to shreds and becomes an obsessing *idée-force*. The mind threatens the naïve man with inflation. . . . The danger becomes greater the more the outer object captivates our interest and the more man forgets that, hand in hand with the differentiation of our connection with nature, there should also go a similar differentiation of our relation to the mind, in order to create the necessary equilibrium.[93]

Without a doubt Descartes was in danger of identifying with his scientific discovery and of overlooking the autonomous

nature of his experience. (Just think of his "*Cogito ergo sum*"—
"*I* think, therefore *I* am"![94]) According to his view, all bodily
reactions, as well as the feelings and the sense perceptions, can
be separated from the ego—as it happens, for instance, in the
dream—but thinking cannot be thus abstracted. He says:
"Cogitare? Hic invenio: cogitatio: *haec sola a* me divelli ne-
quit." ("To think? Here I discover: Thinking! This alone
cannot be taken from me.")[95] Thinking is thus the function of
consciousness par excellence, which is completely unified with
the ego[96] (and for Descartes the soul consists only of the
thinking ego[97]). In other words, Descartes identifies completely with his thinking function.[98] But for this very reason
he is in danger of overlooking the "autonomous" nature of his
thinking experience; and therefore the "mind" in its primordial form haunts him most terrifyingly in the night. Also in
these phantoms there probably lies hidden all that still sur-
passes his own comprehension concerning his discovery:[99] the
archetypal processes in the background and the dawn of a new
spirit of the time, with its dangerous trends, threatening the
human order of things. Was not this precisely the time of the
outbreak of the Thirty Years' War, whose consequences were
destined to destroy all culture in the heart of Europe for a long
time to come?[100]

The word *ghosts*, moreover, evokes the thought of the dead.
Here we may remember that Descartes's mother died when he
was still an infant. For him the image of the mother remained
in the Beyond, and he was doomed to forego the maternal
warmth and protection which a child needs to enable him to
turn away from the world of images of the collective unconscious and face life. Hence, in his case, undoubtedly a door
had remained open into the world of spirits, the land of the
dead. No doubt this is why he was never able to project the
anima onto a real woman. When the mother dies so early, she
often leaves a great secret yearning in her son, so that, as Jung
explains, no other woman can attain to the figure—the more
powerful for being so distant—of the mother.

> The more distant and unreal the personal mother, the more
> profoundly does the longing for her move the son in the depths

of his soul, there to awaken the primordial and eternal image of
the mother, for which reason everything that is containing,
protective, nourishing, and helpful takes on for us the form of
the mother. . . .[101]

In Descartes's case these mothers were the Mater Ecclesia and
Science, the latter of which he often compared with a chaste
woman.[102]

To connect these ghosts with the unrealized background of
his scientific discovery, on the one hand, and with the image
of the mother and the anima, on the other, is not as inconsis-
tent as might appear at first sight: Descartes's simplification of
mathematics and the fact that he exalted the latter as the only
valid means of representing physical processes contributed
together with the works of Kepler, Galileo, and others,[103] most
definitely toward the building-up of a new, purely mechanistic
conception of the world, which remained valid up till the end
of the nineteenth century. But what was lost at the time, as W.
Pauli has shown, [104] was the oneness of the reality which
included the observer; also lost was the ancient doctrine of
correspondence, in which the psychic factor and the idea of a
meaningful teleological order in nature still had a place. Descartes definitely denied the existence of a *causa finalis* in natural
events.[105] As Pauli points out further [106]—with reference to
Kepler's theories—it was really the image (among other things)
of an objectively existing *anima mundi* ("world-soul") and of
an objective psychic factor in general which was discarded at
that time—which, in other words, became unconscious. The
image of the Trinity was projected into the material world and
was sought for there, while the fourth principle was lost once
again.[107] With Kepler, the three-dimensional character of space
is an image of the Trinity, and the mathematical laws of nature
are the laws in the mind of God; with Descartes, the veracity
and immutable stability of God guarantee the regularity of the
physical laws of movement.[108] In his *Principia* (2.37) Descartes
says that this is first law of nature:

Each thing, insofar as it is simple and undivided, always remains
as much as possible in the same state and never changes but by

external causes. . . . A second law is that each part of matter, regarded in itself, does not tend ever to continue moving along curved lines. . . . The cause of the latter law is the same as that of the former one, namely, the immutability of God and the simplicity of operation whereby He conserves motion in matter. . . . Through this immutability of His workings God maintains the world in exactly the state in which He first created it.

The knowledge of the simple physical laws of the movement of matter suffice, therefore, fully to explain all natural phenomena.[109] The possibility that God could have a trickster-aspect or could deceive or behave irrationally or acausally is to Descartes unthinkable.[110] God, on the contrary, guarantees that nature obeys laws and also guarantees the clear and distinct ideas in men's minds, which thus constitute an organon for investigating the physical world.[111] He says in *Meditation* I: "Generally we can certainly assert that God can do everything which we are able to comprehend, but not that he cannot do what we cannot understand." ("Et généralement nous pouvons bien assurer que Dieu peut faire tout ce que nous pouvons comprendre, mais non pas qu'il ne peut faire ce que nous ne pouvons pas comprendre.") He can, indeed, act differently, but He *will* not do so. As Barth formulates it: "God's acts of will clothe themselves with the laws of the pure conceptions of nature; they coincide with intellectual order."[112]

For Descartes the inner "logic" of physical events is thus completely identical with the inner "logic" of our own thinking.[113] As with Spinoza, the course of our thinking (*ordo et connexio idearum*) is the same as that of physical events (*ordo et connexio rerum sive corporum*).[114] Wolfgang Röd[115] has convincingly worked out this practical (or should one, perhaps, go so far as to call it concretistic?) foundation of Cartesian thinking and has shown how greatly Descartes hoped thereby to arrive at certainty concerning his philosophical and even moral views. For him physical determinism thus almost became a proof of God's existence, for the causal chains of psychic and physical events originate in God as the *causa prima*,[116] and, as Felsch stresses,[117] Descartes also attributed an ordered working to

God, that is, to the metaphysical origins, and only made a few concessions to the freedom of God for reasons of theological prudence. We may therefore conclude that *for him the activity of God is essentially identical with the principle of causality*. He was thus himself aware that the principle of causality belongs to the *notiones communes* or inborn *veritates aeternae*.[118] Felsch lays stress here on the correspondence with Kant, who likewise held that causality belongs to the "categories of pure reason."

Descartes held the view that the working of causality has nothing to do with time;[119] for him time itself is a discontinuous series of moments (instants).[120]

It is thus significant that the dreams portray their essential quality by means of ghostly phenomena or parapsychological events. If the unconscious brings up such phenomena in a dream, it wishes to impress the existence of these facts upon the dreamer. Such phenomena are, however, as Jung has shown in his paper on synchronicity,[121] acausal happenings, in which an outer physical event coincides in a meaningful way with a psychically constellated content but cannot be seen as having a causal connection with it. Descartes did not see this principle of synchronicity and in fact rejected its contemporary parallel conception, the doctrine of *correspondentia*. He even excluded it from his thinking.[122] His one-sided and exclusive acceptance of the laws of causality engendered a lack of clarity in his system concerning the relation of soul and body, which lack one of his pupils, Arnold Geulinex,[123] tried to clarify by introducing the idea that the two factors run parallel to each other, like two watches wound up at the same time.[124]

Descartes surmised that the connection between body and soul was to be sought in the experience of the "*passiones*" (emotions as psychological events);[125] we are reminded that, according to Jung, synchronistic phenomena are especially apt to take place when an archetypal content has been constellated and, with it, a state of emotional tension in the observer. But Descartes was not able to clarify the idea of the mediating *passiones* or to bring it into relation to his views of the physical world.[126] As a consequence he shuts out not only the anima but also the problems of evil and the irrational.

In this illuminating night of terror the unconscious certainly seeks to set precisely this area of facts and problems before Descartes in an impressive fashion, but he does not grasp it. Instead, in the first terrified moment of waking, he thinks of "the influence of evil spirits," though he does not go into this idea more profoundly.

Seen in this connection, it is understandable that Descartes, in the first terrified moment of waking from his dream, should think that evil spirits had been at work; for not only has he excluded the anima from his picture of the world, but he has also shut out the problem of evil as well as the element of the irrational.

The appearance of the ghosts is the cause for, or coincides with, the fact that Descartes thinks he is walking through streets; he is thrown out of his established introverted life in his room and driven into collective life—a compensation for his fear of entering the life of ordinary human beings.[127] Over and beyond this it is an impulse to strive after collective aims, as yet unknown to him. Furthermore, his fear compels him to bend low down on the left (or throw himself over onto the left side?).[128] This likewise should be understood in the first place as a compensation; the unconscious wants to force him over to the left, onto the *sinister* ("left"), feminine side, which he is far too fond of overlooking and undervaluing.[129]

It is fear which causes Descartes to bend over to the left. Strangely enough, the ghosts do not appear on the left (where, speaking mythologically, they would seem to belong) but on the right, apparently because on the right there was a weak spot, an open door to the contents of the unconscious. Since the unconscious thrusts him over to the left, it is evident that of himself he has a tendency to diverge too much to the right, which likewise corresponds to a certain *unconsciousness*—for consciousness is a phenomenon of the center, between instinct and spirit. In his "On the Nature of the Psyche,"[130] Jung compares conscious psychic life to a ray of light which spreads into a spectrum, one end of which represents the urges and instincts, namely, the psychoid life processes, which gradually go over into the chemical processes of the body, while the other consists of the (equally psychoid) archetypal contents, the element of the spirit.[131] Both poles ultimately transcend consciousness. In this sense one might say that Descartes, through his somewhat compulsive meditation, had come too close to the spiritual pole and had thus become too unconscious on this side (in other words, he was in danger of being possessed by archetypal contents). Therefore, he felt "a great weakness" on the right side, and the dream motif endeavors to rectify the situation by taking him over to the left.[132] Moreover, it compels him to bend down low as a balance for his somewhat inflated "enthusiasm" (as Maritain emphasizes, he actually considered himself to be *the* man called upon to reform the entire science of his day).[133]

Ashamed, he nevertheless tries to walk upright, only to feel himself seized by a fierce whirlwind that spins him round on his left foot. The ghosts have now transformed themselves into the πνεῦμα (pneuma or divine spirit), into a storm which theatens him. This spirit whirls him around just at the moment when he endeavors to stand upright: "Take care not to spit *against* the wind!"[134] The man of the Renaissance, who casts off his medieval humility and, raising himself, begins to trust his own thinking—this is the man who is caught by the destructive storm, which had already begun to blow in a threatening way in the "Brothers of the Free Spirit," the "Friends of God on the Rhine," the "Tertiaries," and other Holy Ghost movements.[135] This whirlwind may have to do with the "storm" of the Reformation and the Counter-Reformation, which is beginning to break up the ancient order of things in Germany, where Descartes is now living. The storm tells us that the ghosts in the first dream undoubtedly belonged to the host of the dead, the host of the wild huntsman, Wotan.[136] Descartes is among those who were seized by the new spirit; his discoveries help open the way for the establishment of another *Weltanschauung,* that of a newly dawning age, characteristic of which is the development, on the one hand, of scientific thinking but, on the other, of the growth of a pernicious *hubris* of consciousness for which later generations will have to pay. The left side is again characterized as helpful; only on his left foot is Descartes still able to maintain his standpoint on earth, but even so the wind whirls him round three or four times (!) in a circle.

This whirling causes him to turn on his own axis, so that he has to look in all the directions of the compass in turn—a compensation for his one-sided point of view. The unconscious is aiming at a widening of his horizon and a shifting of the center of rotation from the outer world into his own sphere. This image of the whirlwind also appears to be projected into Descartes's cosmogonic theory, according to which the world proceeds from a continuously expanding equal diffusion of extended matter in which the small spheres of the four primal elements fall into a spiral movement and begin to rotate around themselves and around certain outer central points, which are now the stars.[137] As Fleckenstein remarks, these bizarre Cartesian vortices constitute "the first effort in the direction of a continuum physics."[138] In themselves creation myths are representations from the unconscious of the emergence of consciousness, so that from Descartes's own theory one might conclude that these spiral movements in the dream could mean the inception of an awakening new consciousness.

There is a noteworthy detail in the fact that Descartes is whirled around *three or four* times. The problematical relation of three to four is precisely *the* psychologically significant matter, which is already expressed in the alchemistic axiom of Maria Prophetissa, "One becomes two, two becomes three, and out of the third comes the one as the fourth."[139] "This uncertainty," comments Jung,

> has a duplex character—in other words, the central ideas are ternary as well as quaternary. The psychologist cannot but mention the fact that a similar puzzle exists in the psychology of the unconscious: the least differentiated or "inferior" function[140] is so much contaminated by the collective unconscious that, on becoming conscious, it brings up the archetype of the Self as well—τὸ ἓν τέταρτον, as Maria Prophetissa says. Four signifies the feminine, motherly, physical; three the mas-

culine, fatherly, spiritual. Thus the uncertainty as to three or four amounts to a wavering between the spiritual and the physical. . . .

As already mentioned, that is precisely *the* problem for Descartes, who tore the physical and the psychic apart with his causal thinking and its corresponding mechanistic view of the world and who was unable to integrate the fourth—the feminine and maternal—into his personal life. It might be possible to object here that too many motifs are pulled into the detailed interpretation of the dream, but, after all, the dream *does* exactly state—and this is typical for such "big dreams"—that Descartes is whirled around three or four times, neither more nor less.[141] It might be further mentioned that the names "Descartes" was originally "de Quartis"!

While he is being whisked around to such an extent, Descartes is tormented by a constant fear of falling, of touching the earth, that is, reality, the maternal/feminine. He then notices a college, which stands open, and resolves to seek help and protection by offering up a prayer in its chapel. As Maritain stresses, this place might well be connected with the Jesuit college of La Flèche, in which Descartes grew up,[142] and would therefore represent the spiritual training and the whole framework of orthodox conceptions in himself, by means of which—like so many others at the time of the Counter-Reformation—he sought to save himself from being possessed by the new spirit (at the time of the dream he was serving in the army of Maximilian of Bavaria). The storm is blowing in the direction of the church, so it cannot be the wind that once filled the early church. It is rather a storm which has its origin not *in* the Church but *outside* it. It "bloweth where it listeth," and the church is no longer its vessel but, according to circumstances, either an obstacle on its path or a refuge for those who fear the wind. The situation at that time could hardly be more aptly represented symbolically! Descartes himself was puzzled by this paradox: he interpreted the wind as "the evil spirit which tried to push him forcibly to a place where he wanted to go voluntarily" ("le mauvais génie qui tâchait le jeter par

force dans un lieu où son dessein étoit d'aller volontaire-
ment").[143] A marginal note adds:

A malo Spiritu ad Templum propellebar: C'est pourquoi Dieu
ne permit pas qu'il avançât plus loin et qu'il se laissât emporter,
même en un lieu saint, par un Esprit qu'il n'avait pas envoyé:
quoy qu'il fût très-persuadé, que c'eût été l'Esprit de Dieu qui
luy avoit fait faire les premières démarches vers cette Église.[144]

(I was pushed by an evil spirit toward the church: This is why
God did not allow him [Descartes] to go further and be carried
away—even into a holy place—by a spirit which He had not
sent, though he [Descartes] was completely convinced that it
had first been the spirit of God who made him take the first
steps toward that Church.)

Descartes is quite naturally in doubt as to whether this wind is
the spirit of God or the spirit of Satan, which was also thought
to be a *ventus urens,* coming out of the North.[145] Descartes's
uncertainty concerning the moral significance of the storm
may be compared with the doubt experienced by Saint Ignatius
of Loyola when, in a profoundly beneficial vision, he saw a
snake "which was full of luminous eyes, although they were
really not eyes."[146] Later, however, he concluded that it must
be a diabolical apparition.[147] Saint Niklaus von der Flüe also
had subsequently to tone down his terrifying vision of God,
for the personal experience of it almost disrupted him.[148] This,
too, is a somewhat similar case; in itself the storm is a morally
unbiased image, emerging spontaneously from the unconscious and symbolizing a primordial experience of the spirit
whose effects could be various: he who allowed himself to be
carried away by it stormed against the Church, whereas he
who fled was bound to dig himself into the Church, with
windows and doors tight shut, and could not leave it and go
about freely again without danger. Few indeed had sufficient
humility to bend low down toward the earth—certainly not
Descartes, and therefore he decided subsequently to explain
the storm as the work of the evil spirit.
In his haste, however, he notices that he has passed an

acquaintance without greeting him, but when he endeavors to go back and make good this omission, the wind stops him. Unfortunately, we lack any associations or statements which might tell us who this Mr. N. might be and are therefore unable to discover what role he played in Descartes's psyche;[149] but he was evidently a man for whom Descartes must have had a positive feeling or a certain respect, since he regretted not having greeted him. We can only say, therefore, that the "acquaintance" represents a part of Descartes's personality which, in his state of enthusiasm, he is in danger of overlooking. The unusual gift which this young man of only twenty-three possessed in the realm of thinking—amounting indeed to creative genius—obviously suggests that he developed in a very one-sided way and in a measure far outran his own nature, leaving parts of his personality undeveloped behind him. Moreover, his natural inclination to escape life and his fear of love involvements, as well as his skepticism, encouraged still further this one-sided development of his introverted thinking.

We know that, at the time of the dream, Descartes was making a particular effort to become conscious of his own thinking; so we may assume that the aspect of the personality which he negligently passes by is connected with his emotions and his feeling side and, in a wider sense, is bound up with his undifferentiated fourth function. It may therefore not be misleading to surmise a shadow-figure of Descartes in Mr. N., which nonetheless has a rather positive meaning for him and which he had only overlooked, not rejected. It would be interesting to know what Descartes said in his lost treatise "De genio Socratis"; for in Socrates' case, too, there was a really split personality, connected with the pronounced cabiric traits exhibited by his *daimonion*. Descartes was probably interested in Socrates because he projected his own problem onto him. He also speaks of the fact that *"le génie"* gave him notice in advance of the great dream.[150] It is not clear exactly what he meant by his *"génie"*; he probably conceived of it, as Sirven surmises, as a kind of *spiritus familiaris* or *"cousin de l'ange gardien."*[151]

In the dream Descartes does, certainly, try to make up for

his fault; but then he comes up against the wind. The attempt to compensate would have been a step toward the attainment of inner wholeness; but precisely at such a moment the whole resistance of collective trends makes itself felt. This confrontation with the *Zeitgeist,* demanding an effort to come to terms with it and an individual self-assertion in face of it, is a step which, as his biography shows, Descartes never uncompromisingly attempted. Did he himself not say, speaking of his appearance in the world, *"Larvatus prodeo"* ("[Only] with a mask do I appear in public!").[152] But it is not only outwardly that he avoided any risk of disclosing himself; inwardly, as well, he remained curiously undecided in regard to the most critical religious questions of his time and in the personal conduct of his life. The lack of a mother deprived him of the vitality and rooted contact with the earth which would have enabled him to maintain himself against the storm.

Even so, his attempt to reach Mr. N., who has been left behind, brings about a positive change in the dream: in the college quadrangle another man calls to him, saying that, if he is going in quest of Mr. N., he would like to give him something for him, and Descartes thinks the object is a melon, which has been brought from an exotic land.

The church as a spiritual shelter has somehow disappeared from Descartes's field of vision in the dream, but in its stead the college quadrangle still serves him as a maternal, sheltering "temenos."[153] The college quadrangle represents the rigid spiritual training which Descartes had received at the hands of the Jesuit fathers and which never ceased to color his entire philosophy.[154] The people within this frame are all able to stand quietly upright; he alone continues to be hampered by the wind.

He is one "possessed," one who has been touched by the *Zeitgeist.* Here the dream emphasizes his individual situation. The unknown man whom Descartes meets in the college quadrangle might well represent the side of himself which has still remained completely within the framework of the spirit of the Church—a figure who stands for the traditional spirit or for the Catholic in him. It has often been pointed out, and with justice, that somewhere within himself Descartes cherished a kind of rigid, static belief, something quite separate from his living intellectual spiritual search—a "fides *non* quaerens intellectum" ("a faith which does *not* seek understanding"), as Maritain so trenchantly puts it.[155] Very likely it is this aspect of Descartes that is embodied by the man in the quadrangle. This man gives him an interesting mission: He must take something to Mr. N.—and Descartes thinks in the dream that it is a melon.

Hence between Mr. N., who has been passed by in the street, and the man in the college quadrangle there is evidently a connection, a sort of system of barter or trading in presents, in which Descartes is called upon to play in instrumental role. Evidently this inner side in Descartes, which has "remained behind," is still to a great extent maintained by the traditional spirit of the college. Mr. N., as already mentioned, stands for an unconscious part of the personality but one which—and this is significant—does not coincide with the Catholic in him, for in the dream he appears outside the "framework" of the church, in the street, in the collective, profane sphere. So he might possibly represent an unchristian shadow-figure. Since Descartes never troubled about this unconscious part of his personality, it must have got its nourishment elsewhere, presumably from the college. This may perhaps be connected with the fact that, whenever attacked, Descartes always sought the help of his old schoolmasters, Père Charlet and Père Dinet. Since, as a personality, he was never inwardly united and never had his shadow with him, he lacked the strength to face the spiritual battle of his time.

The object which Descartes has to take Mr. N. is really rather unexpected: a melon, which, he presumes, must have been brought from an exotic land.

In the East, as in Africa and southern Europe, the melon has an important symbolic meaning. It was already known in the West and in the Mediterranean regions in antiquity and had probably spread from Egypt in all directions.[156] As early as the time of Moses, melons were among the fruits for the sake of which the children of Israel hankered after the land of Egypt:

And the mixed multitude that was among them fell a-lusting: and the children of Israel also wept again, and said, Who shall give us flesh to eat? We remember the fish, which we did eat in Egypt freely; the cucumbers, and the melons, and the leeks, and the onions, and the garlic: But now our soul is dried away: there is nothing at all, besides this manna, before our eyes. [157]

This passage is important insofar as in the patristic literature the departure of the Jews from Egypt is understood as a breaking away from polytheistic pagan unconsciousness. [158] Melons are consequently the much-loved food of the *pagan shadow* of the Jews, or else of the Christians. This is significant, because we have speculated that Mr. N. might have represented a non-Christian shadow of Descartes. This passage from the Bible would, moreover, have been known to Descartes.

In the Greek sphere of culture the melon is called πέπων ("ripe, completely cooked"; also a pet name for children). In a scholium it is called *spermatias*, [159] probably on account of its abundance of seeds. To distinguish it from the watermelon, the round edible melon was specially known as μηλοπέπων ("quince-apple") [160] on account of its apple-like shape (*mēlon* = apple). This is the origin of the Latin word *melo, melonis* and of our word "melon." It was already a matter of wonder to the ancients why this fruit in particular should be called "ripe," as all fruit presumably deserves that name. [161] It was prized for the amount of water it contained and for its refreshing and aperient effect. [162] In medieval popular medicine its seeds, cooked in milk, were used as a remedy for phthisis. [163] This is worth mentioning, inasmuch as Descartes suffered from weak lungs and died of inflammation of the lungs (contracted in Sweden's cold, stormy, northern winter).

In the Chinese imagery of the *I Ching*, [164] the oracular *Book of Changes*, the melon is symbolized by the sign *ch'ien*, "heaven," because *ch'ien* is round. But it is emphasized that the melon spoils easily and therefore belongs to the feminine principle of darkness, Yin. The image of "a melon covered with willow leaves" is therefore interpreted as "hidden lines— then it drops down to one from heaven." [165] "Hidden lines" means in China a pattern of the Tao which man does not yet know and which, when it becomes suddenly conscious to him after a ripening process in the unconscious, is compared with the falling of a ripe fruit from above. So the oracle evidently means that *the melon represents a latent conscious order within the darkness, which suddenly and unexpectedly becomes manifest.*

The main theme of this whole section of the *I Ching* depicts the unexpected meeting of a bold and shameless girl who associates with five men, for which reason, we are told, one should not marry her.[166] The commentary continues:

> However, things that must be avoided in human society have meaning in the processes of nature. Here the meeting of earthly and heavenly forces is of great significance, because at the moment when the earthly force enters and the heavenly force is at its height—in the fifth month—all things unfold to the high point of their material manifestation, and the dark forces cannot injure the light force.

According to the commentary this dark Yin principle is, however, *symbolized by the melon.* The melon thus connects here with the image of a dark hetaeristic anima, who still displays a piece of unadulterated and unassimilable nature, which is dangerous for the conventional human order. (Descartes's liaison with Helena Jans comes to mind.) This connection of the symbol of the melon with the image of the anima is due to the fact that it is a very watery fruit, and water is a widespread symbol for the living essence of the psyche.[167] The old alchemists never tired of devising new and expressive synonyms for this water. They called it *aqua nostra, mercurius vivus, argentum vivum, vinum ardens, aqua vitae, succus lunariae,* and so on, by which they meant a living being not devoid of substance, as opposed to the rigid immateriality of mind in the abstract.[168] The expression *succus lunariae* ("sap of the moon plant") points exactly enough to the nocturnal origin of the water, and *aqua nostra,* like *mercurius vivus,* to its earthliness. *Acetum fontis* is a powerful corrosive water that dissolves all created things and at the same time leads to the most durable of all products, the mysterious *lapis* ("stone").[169] These alchemistic amplifications will prove not to be so far-fetched as they might at first appear; this watery element in the melon undoubtedly hints at the anima and the problem of evil, as can be shown even more clearly in a Japanese fairy tale, "Princess Melon,"[170] which runs as follows:

> An old childless couple lived alone in the mountains. While the woman was washing in the river, she saw a huge melon floating toward her from the upper reaches of the stream and took it home. When the old people cut it open, they found inside it a wonderfully beautiful tiny girl, whom they called "Princess Melon." She grew up to be a sagacious and beautiful maiden. One day when the old couple went off to a village festivity and she was minding the house on her own, the evil demon Amanojaku came and dragged her away and bound her to a plum tree in the garden. He then took on her form and sat himself in her place. But she succeeded in calling out to her homecoming parents, telling them what had happened, so that they were able to kill the demon.

According to another version, the demon devours the princess but is then convicted of the murder and executed; and it is the blood he sheds that dyes the millet flowers so red.

In connection with the foregoing associations to the dream, it is important that this melon-spirit originated in the water ("washed up by the stream of life and of happenings") and that she secretly drew to herself an evil demon because she possessed a similar dark background. This melon-princess recalls one of the central motifs of a group of European fairy tales of the type of "The Three Lemons" (or oranges):[171] A prince seeks a beautiful wife and with the help of a little old woman finds a lemon tree by a spring. Three times he cuts a fruit off; each time a beautiful woman immediately appears and says: "Give me something to drink." Only at the third attempt does he succeed in giving it to her quickly enough so that she does not die, as did the first two women, but stands before him in her naked beauty. He allows her to hide herself in a tree while he fetches her clothes. But during his absence she is discovered by an evil Moorish woman (cook, witch, etc.) who kills her and puts herself in the victim's place. The dead woman reappears as a dove, is killed once again, and from her blood grows a lemon tree. When the prince once again opens one of its fruits, she steps forth redeemed, and the Moorish woman is punished. Here, too, the anima[172] is concealed in the round yellow fruit; and like the melon-princess, she, too, attracts a correspondingly dark, chthonic figure that, for men, constellates the problem of the confrontation with evil.

This problem of evil leads over to a further meaning of the melon. As the ritual food of those known as the *electi*,[173] this fruit plays a symbolically significant role in Manichaeism. The whole meaning and purpose of the Manichaean way of life is to save the "germs of light" imprisoned in darkness and convey them back to the original realm of light. Plants and trees are particularly rich in these germs of light; in them lives the *anima passibilis* of the Savior (that aspect of the soul of the Savior which was capable of suffering), "who is crucified in every tree."[174] Plants and human bodies contain the greatest number of these germs of light because they have their origin in the seeds of the Archons, the planetary gods who compose Yaldabaoth's following. The *electi*, the higher adepts among the Manichaeans, were therefore strictly vegetarian; they ate only plants containing a large quantity of these germs of light, among which cucumbers and melons are especially mentioned. The aim was to store up the element of light contained in such fruit in the body—which lived a chaste life—and thus withdraw it from the process of procreation. In a small way the *electi* were, like the water wheel of the cosmos,[175] a sort of machine for saving the element of light; through their digestion they set free the particles of light, and at their death these returned to the realm of light.[176]

The pleasant taste and smell of the melon, as well as its beautiful color, are doubtless the reason why (according to Saint Augustine) it belonged to the "golden treasures of God."[177] As a light-containing fruit it recalls the role of the apple of Paradise, the partaking of which mediated to humanity the knowledge of good and evil that had until then belonged only to God. The apple really contains in embryo the possibility of becoming conscious, the γνῶσις θεοῦ ("cognitive experience of God"), through the understanding of the opposites of good and evil contained within Him. Descartes would fairly certainly have known of the Manichaean significance of the melon, since he was acquainted with Augustine's work *De Genesi contra Manichaeos*[178] and therefore would probably also have read his further treatises against the Manichaeans, which were usually printed with it. It might therefore be assumed that for him the melon, like the apple of Paradise, could have signified an attempt to ponder more deeply over the problem of good and evil and, in contradistinction to the ecclesiastical conception of evil as a *privatio boni* ("privation of good"),[179] to participate in the Manichaean recognition of the divine reality of evil. At that time he felt himself oppressed by a *"mauvais génie,"* but he did not subsequently face up to the problem more deeply on the philosophical level. It is certainly no accident that he dreamt of this Manichaean symbol and, on first waking, as he himself records, "for two hours had many thoughts about the good and evil of this world." The image of the melon actually suggests the idea of an achievement of consciousness based on an experience of life—through the acceptance of the anima and of the conflict of good and evil. This image is at the same time the feminine, which mediated between Descartes's ecclesiastical element and his nonecclesiastical inner side.

The Manichaean idea of the liberation of the germs of light is also to be found in various Gnostic systems. The Sethians, for instance, advocated the following doctrine.[180] The All consists of Three Principles (ἀρχαί): the Light above, the Darkness below, and, in between, a pure, sweet-scented Pneuma. The Light shone forth in the Darkness, which was a "terrible water," which thereafter strove to hold onto the germs of light by means of the scent of the Pneuma. But the powers of these three primordial principles (δυνάμεις) were infinite, "each one rational and capable of thought" (φρόνιμοι καὶ νοεραί). They collided, and their collision was "like the impression of a seal";[181] and since there were endless numbers of these powers, endless collisions took place, and countless impressions (εἰκόνες) of endless seals resulted.[182] Thus the Cosmos in its multiplicity came into being. Each part of the Cosmos is, however, a monad which recapitulates the whole Cosmos in miniature. The perfume of the Pneuma, which floated up together with the light, now sown in this infinity (as σπινθὴρ φωτός, "spark of light"), and *a mighty generating wind,*[183] *which gave rise to all things,* rose up out of the primal waters and whipped up its waves, which became pregnant and caught hold of the light that, together with the Pneuma, had been scattered down. This is only a small (trifling) spark,[184] "like a piece separated from a ray of light, which is brought down into the multifariously combined, mixed, physical world and 'calls out from many waters' (Psalm 29:3)." The thinking and aspirations of the upper Light proceed toward the redemption, once again, of this spirit,[185] and for this reason Man, too, must exert himself in the same direction.

Another (Ophitic) sect describes the creation of the world in the following manner:[186] the Father and Primal man is a Light that lives holy and ageless in the power of the βυθός ("abyss"). From him proceeds the Ennoia ("Thought, Reflection") as the Son and second man; beneath him lies the Pneuma; and still farther below are Darkness, Chaos, Water, and the Abyss, above which hovers the spirit, the first woman. From this woman the Father engendered the third man, Christ. The woman, however, cannot endure the greatness of her light and rushes and flies over to the left, down to the earthly world. This light streaming toward the left possesses a dew of light in which the Prunikos (i.e., the "left one") is enveloped and is flung down, and it strives to raise itself up again with the help of this dew of light. The consummation will take place when the complete dew of light is gathered up and changed into the everlasting Aion.[187] The idea of the light lost in matter also appears here.

The "Barbelo" Gnostics taught the following.[188] From the primal Father proceeds Barbelo (possibly, "Out of the Four comes God"). But her son Yaldabaoth (or Sabaoth, the Lord of the Seventh Heaven) becomes arrogant and declares himself

to be the only God. Barbelo weeps over his trespass "and now
appears before the Archons (gods of the planets, who formed
Yaldabaoth's following) in a ravishing form and robs them of
their seed through their ejaculation in order by this means to
bring their powers, which were scattered in many creatures,
back to herself."[189] This is the reason why man must also
withdraw his procreative power or his semen from the earthly
process of becoming and guide it, once more, to the divine.
Leisegang remarks:

> From this we can understand the passage from the "Gospel of
> Eve," quoted by Epiphanius:[190] "I stood on a high mountain and
> saw a vast man and another shrunken figure, God the Father
> with Barbelo, who is shriveled up because her power has been
> taken from her; and I heard something like a voice of thunder,
> and I came closer in order to hear, and it spoke to me and said:
> 'I am thee and thou art me, and where thou art, there am I, and
> I am sown in all things. And when thou wilt, gather me up;
> when, however, thou gatherest me, thou gatherest thyself.' "[191]

This gathering of the power was then symbolically expressed
through their spermatic union, which they also conceived of
as a "fruitfulness" of the body. For them redemption consisted
in uniting their seed with the procreative substance of the
universe, that is, withdrawing it from its earthly destiny and
leading it back to the divine original source of all seed.[192]

Closely allied spiritually with the Manichaean ideas is the
doctrine of the Gnostic Basilides. According to him the
"nonbeing" (potential) God first creates a seed of the Cosmos;[193] "just as the seed of mustard contains, at the same time,
everything comprised in the smallest space . . . ," so this
unmanifest seed comprises the seed-entirety of the Cosmos. In
this sperm sojourns the "thrice-divided sonship," of which the
finest element straightway hastens back to the Father above
and the second element also hurries aloft again, borne on the
wings of the Pneuma. Only the third part, "in need of cleans-
ing," remains below, caught in the mass of the cosmic entirety
of seeds, and "does good and allows good to be done to it."[194]
This third sonship has still to be redeemed through the process

known as φυλοκρίνησις, the separation of the natures.[195] Here, too, man must cooperate in bringing this power of God, that is ensnared in matter, back to its realm up above. The Manichaean idea of the salvation of the germs of light is made clearer by the help of these Gnostic parallels. According to the Manichaean conception these germs are contained especially in cucumbers, melons, and similar fruit, whose mass of seeds probably suggested the idea of a *thesaurus* or totality of seeds.[196] A transverse section of both these fruits yields the design of a mandala,[197] which certainly also explains the Manichaean meaning of the melon as a "golden treasure" of God: it is a symbol of the Self. It is not by chance that its Greek name also emphasizes its round (applelike) form, which resembles the images of psychic totality, of the Self.[198]

The symbol of the melon could be compared with the "round body of light" of the alchemists, which they also describe as "yolk of egg" or "the red point of the sun in the middle."[199] It is an image similar to the one which the alchemist Gerhard Dorn describes as the "infallible center of the middle." Commenting on this idea, Jung says:

> The point in the center is the fire. Upon it is based the simplest and completest form, which is what the roundness is. The point comes closest to the nature of the light, and the light is a *simulacrum Dei*. The firmament was created in the midst of the waters, so to speak . . . ; in man too there is a *lucidum corpus,* namely, the *humidum radicale,* which stems from the sphere of the waters above the firmament. This corpus is the sidereal balsam which maintains the body heat. . . . The *corpus lucens* is the *corpus astrale,* the firmament or star in man.[200]

These amplifications from Paracelsus's range of thought seem to me to be enlightening about the melon as well.

The green network on a melon looks like the lines of meridian on a globe of the world, so it is obvious to look upon the melon as a sort of microcosmos. It is an image of the inner "firmament," of the psychic totality, that is here brought forth by the unconscious as a counterbalance to the phenomena of the macrocosm, which had so greatly fascinated Descartes.[201]

In this instance the *"rotundum"* is manifestly a fruit, whereby the Self is described as something that has grown naturally, the result of a quiet process of ripening. It is a symbol of a light and an order which, however, ripens in the darkness of natural creation. As Jung demonstrates in his article "The Philosophical Tree,"[202] tree and plant motifs have an important meaning, which is greatly clarified by amplifications from the realm of alchemy. In the "Visio Arislei,"[203] for instance, a precious tree is mentioned whose fruit satisfies the hunger of mankind forever, like the *panis vitae* ("bread of life") of John 6:35. The sun- and moon-trees of the "Legend of Alexander" are also often quoted, and Benedictus Figulus equated them with the apple trees in the Garden of the Hesperides and their rejuvenating fruit.[204] The tree symbolizes the entire alchemical opus;[205] at the same time it is also "a metamorphic form of man, so to speak, since it proceeds from the primal man and becomes man."[206] Jung concludes his interpretation of the tree in the following manner:

> Insofar as the tree, both morally and physically (*tam ethice quam physice*), symbolizes the opus and the process of transformation, it is also clear that it indicates the life process in general.[207] Its identity with Mercurius, the *spiritus vegetativus,* confirms this idea. Since the opus represented by the tree is a mystery of life, death, and rebirth, this interpretation also applies to the *arbor philosophica,* as does also the attribute of wisdom; which offers a valuable hint to psychology. Since times long past the tree has served as a symbol of Gnosis and wisdom. Thus Irenaeus says that, for the Barbelites, the tree is born out of man (i.e., the Ἄνθρωπος) and the Gnosis, and these, too, they called Gnosis. In the Gnosis of Justinus the angel of the revelation, Baruch, is designated as τὸ ξύλον τῆς ζωῆς, which reminds us of the future-discerning sun- and moon-trees of the "Legend of Alexander."[208]

But, as Jung explains in another passage, Gnosis means "a perception that wells up from the inner experience, a type of perception that is at the same time a vital experience."[209] Descartes lacked this type of perception because he put too much emphasis on conscious thought and not enough on unconscious inspiration. This is why the unconscious set it before him as a goal.

Melons grow in the shade of the leaves of a ground-growing runner, close-pressed against the earth. (Consider Descartes's compulsion to bend down.) This motif of "growing out of and on the earth" thus strongly emphasizes that for which his shadow was longing: to become caught in earthly reality.

In the dream Descartes thinks that this melon comes from an exotic land. It comes from far away; it is something "strange," of a different nature, unfamiliar. As Jung says, in the beginning the Self often appears as something strange, as the "wholly other," because to the ego it will seem to be completely remote as long as the latter remains caught up in its own fictions.[210] A consciousness like Descartes's, whose interests were so definitely directed toward the outer object, would more particularly have to meet this aspect of the Self, since

> The Self, regarded as the opposite pole of the world, its "abso-
> lutely other," is the *sine qua non* of all empirical knowledge and
> consciousness of subject and object. Only because of this psychic
> "otherness" is consciousness possible at all. Identity does not
> make consciousness possible; it is only separation, detachment,
> and agonizing confrontation that produce consciousness and
> understanding. . . . Even today Western man finds it hard to see
> the psychological necessity for a transcendental subject of cog-
> nition as the opposite pole to the empirical universe, although
> the postulate of a world-confronting Self, at least as a "point of
> reflection," is a logical necessity.[211]

Descartes did, indeed, perceive this necessity logically but did not fully recognize its psychic reality, for which reason the melon appeared in the dream as something strange. Later, he used to wander with delight around the Dutch docks, looking at the curious new imports from overseas, which he also liked to investigate in his secret dissecting room. By this means he sought to discover the manifestations of the *lumen naturale* ("natural light"), in the existence of which he believed, as he also believed in the existence of the revealed light. This natural light is, according to him, the reasonableness of our clear and distinct ideas and of the mechanical laws of nature, which have been created by God and whose regularity is assured.[212] Descartes often, moreover, made use of the image of the seed and the fruit when speaking of the inner process of thought. For instance, in his *Regulae ad directionem Ingenii* (*Rules for the Direction of the Mind*) he says:

> . . . the human mind contains something divine in which the seeds of profitable thoughts are so well sown that they often, even when neglected and stifled through false application, bear spontaneous fruit. This we experience the most easily in arithmetic and geometry. Their discoveries were "spontaneous fruits" which were engendered through the inherent principles of the method . . . ; if they are tended conscientiously, they can achieve full maturity.[213]

Descartes himself interpreted the melon as a symbol "*des charmes de la solitude,*"[214] an interpretation which was evidently suggested by the meaning of πέπων, "secret ripening."[215] This inner ripening of the personality is the compensation for the fact of being overwhelmed and swept along by the storm and torn away from his own nature. In later life Descartes actually strove in this direction, but one thing remained an impossibility for him in this endeavor: to take root in the earth.

In the dream Descartes has to take the melon to Mr. N., whom he had passed by—the part in himself with which the symbol should unite him.[216] One cannot help wondering why this shadow is not able to live simply by the ecclesiastical symbol of Christ and the means of grace which the Church affords. Presumably it is because these symbols of the Self no longer exercise a sufficiently immediate and natural effect to appeal directly to the unconscious parts of the personality. Therefore, although these unconscious parts are still nourished within the framework of the Church, they need "light" in the form of a "natural food,"[217] which, according to the dream, the church actually does give incidentally but which it looks upon as profane.

The symbols of the Self within the framework of ecclesiastical conception are all, for their part, of a "pneuma-like nature," in particular, they are *sine umbra peccati* ("without the shadow of original sin"). The image of Christ or of the Host, for example, incorporates only the light, redemptive aspect of the Self.[218] With these means of grace Descartes's shadow would only be able to raise itself up spiritually, away from the earth, but they cannot help him to root himself. He does not in this way find himself implicated in the physical reality which the Mr. N. within him requires and which would create the correct compensation for his intellectual attitude toward life. This explains the design of the unconscious that Descartes should be instrumental in the proceedings, that *he* should bring the melon to Mr. N. In other words, he should be consciously concerned with the needs of his shadow and bring the latter its food, as a Manichaean *auditor* to the *electus*. In this way he would even be serving the Church in a certain sense, for at that time the Church, blinded by its desire to stem the Reformation, was anxious, as the dream says, to "give away" the natural, individual experience of the Self, presumably as a thing of no use and "exotic," in other words, as strange, foreign, and not belonging, since the Self, as already mentioned, is experienced as being different—as the "wholly other."

Even so, in the first instance the melon is in the possession of the Church, very probably because the unconscious feminine principle is projected onto it. It also, however, represents that natural symbol tradition, taken over from paganism, which still survives within the framework of the church—in the outer court, as the dream so pertinently says—and to which the Manichaean problem also belonged.[219] The man in the quadrangle and Mr. N. are both unconscious parts of Descartes, and it is interesting to see how they wish to be connected through him or by means of his intercession. He must find a place for them in consciousness so that they can unite; at the same time, the melon, which depicts the feminine, acts as the mediating principle or as the "uniting symbol." It might be possible to go so far as to say that, inasmuch as it represents not only the Self but the anima as well, the mediating function of the melon in the dream is not unconnected with the fact that, on awakening, Descartes vowed to go on a pilgrimage to the Madonna of Loretto. Here an attempt at a solution of the tension in the Christian way of life is hinted at which has only now found official expression in the "Declaratio Solemnis" of the "Assumptio Mariae."

In the same moment that Descartes is given the commission of handing over the melon, he notices that he is the only one of the group in the college quadrangle who is unable to stand upright against the wind, although the wind has abated. As has already been suggested, he is one chosen, moved by the *Zeitgeist,* and therefore he must hand on the "round thing," he must turn to the inner ripening of his personality, even if he is alone in doing this.

When Descartes wakes up after the dream, he is greatly oppressed by the thought of his sins and feels himself endangered by the evil spirit. Although—as he says—"in the eyes of men" he had led a spotless life, he knows that he has sinned sufficiently to call all the wrath of heaven down on his head in punishment. It is significant that, like most people who try to interpret their own dreams, he should connect the meaning with his personal life and, as a good Catholic, should at once resort to a sort of self-examination. In so doing, however, he overlooks the deeper meaning of the dream—the problem of the reality of evil—and diverts it into the channel of his conscious thinking. Also, even if he did not altogether understand the dream, it mitigated his inflationary enthusiasm and permitted him somehow to feel the evil in the new intellectual attitude; the dream also stemmed the impetuous outward flow of his thoughts and brought them back to dwell on himself and his own life.

Interpretation of the Second Dream

The next so-called "dream" is no real dream; Descartes hears a sharp explosion like a thunderclap and sees—when already awake—fiery sparks glowing in the room. In most

pagan religions a peal of thunder has a numinous significance.[220] In Germanic mythology it occurs when Thor rides
across the heavens with his team of goats; the thunderbolt of
the Greeks and Romans belongs to the supreme deity, Zeus or
Jupiter, who uses it to frighten his enemies, the Titans, and
human beings possessed by *hubris*. In late antiquity there
existed the so-called "Brontologia," a science which dealt with
the interpretation of thunder. Jupiter can also cause thunder to
resound out of a clear sky as a sign of his approval and assent.[221]
In common parlance, "lightning" and "thunder" stand for
violent outbursts of affect. These frequently accompany the
constellation of archetypal contents, which would also fit in
with Descartes's experience. Although he did not really understand the first dream, it evidently "struck home" and touched
him in his innermost being.

Descartes himself interpreted the *"coup de foudre"* as the
descent of the *"esprit de la vérité."*[222] Lightning, as Jung explains,[223] indicates a sudden enlightenment and change of attitude (*mentis sive animi lapsus in alterum mundum* ["rapture of the
mind or soul into another world"], as Rulandus's alchemistic
lexicon defines it[224]). Jakob Boehme describes the Messiah and
also the "Source-Spirit" Mercurius as thunder.[225] "Of the
innermost birth of the soul," Boehme again says that the
bestial body attains "only a glimpse, just as if it lightened."[226]
Caught in the four spirits, the lightning then stands "in the
midst, as a heart."[227] Or: "For when you strike upon the sharp
part of the stone [cf. Descartes's comparison of the sparks in
the flint], the bitter sting of nature sharpens itself and is stirred
in the highest degree. For Nature is dissipated or *broken asunder*
in the sharpness, so that the *Liberty shines forth as a flash*."[228]
The lightning is the "birth of the Light." In his *Vita longa*
Paracelsus recommends a constantly repeated Distillation of
the Center, or, as Jung explains, an awakening and development of the Self.[229] At the end of the process a "physical flash"
appears, and the flash of Saturn and that of the Sun are
separated from each other, and in this flash appears that which
appertains "to long life."[230] Descartes does not pay attention to
the thunder, which he only later mentions and interprets, but

only to the lightning, the emotional shock. The flash of lightning, on the other hand, he sees as a multitude of sparks.

These fiery sparks recall the alchemistic idea of the *scintillae* or *oculi piscium* ("fishes' eyes"), which Jung has explained in the sixth chapter of his paper "On the Nature of the Psyche."[231] At the primitive level, he says, consciousness is as yet not a unity; in other words, it is not yet centered on a firmly structured ego-complex but flares up here and there, wherever outer or inner experiences, instincts, and affects call it up.[232] The developed ego-complex should also be thought of as surrounded by many small luminosities, which can be demonstrated out of the dreams of modern people as well as in alchemistic symbolism. The alchemists often maintained that the transformative substance (the unconscious) contained many "small white sparks."[233] Heinrich Khunrath explains these as rays or sparks of "the Anima Catholica," the universal soul which is identical with the Spirit of God.[234] (The human mind is also one of these sparks.[235]) They are seeds of light in the Chaos,[236] "sparks of the fire of the soul of the world as pure *Formae rerum essentiales*" ("essential ideal form of things").[237] The idea of the *lumen naturale* in Paracelsus is based on a similar conception,[238] which originates in the inner *astrum* or "firmament" in man and is a light that is bestowed on the "inward man."[239] The light of nature is "kindled by the Holy Ghost"[240] and is an "invisible light," an invisible wisdom which is "learned," among other ways, through dreams.[241] Paracelsus's student Gerhard Dorn also held to the doctrine of the *scintillae* which are perceived by the spiritual eyes, shining resplendently.[242] According to Paracelsus the natural light is also innate in animals,[243] for which idea he is indebted to Agrippa von Nettesheim, who speaks of a *"luminositas sensus naturae"* (the light or consciousness immanent in instinctual nature).[244] This is especially worth mentioning, since Descartes had evidently read Agrippa. As Jung explains, these alchemical *scintillae* are descriptions of the archetypes of the collective unconscious, which must accordingly possess a certain inherent luminosity or autonomous latent element of consciousness.[245]

Among the many sparks, the seedlike luminosities of the contents that shine forth out of the darkness of the unconscious, the alchemistic authors often emphasized *one light* as being central and of peculiar importance.[246] In Khunrath this is designated as Monas or Sun,[247] in Gerhard Dorn as *sol invisibilis* ("invisible sun").[248] Many more examples of this conception, to which I should like to refer, are quoted by Jung from numerous other alchemistic and Gnostic sources.[249] In conclusion he says:

> Since consciousness is characterized from of old by expressions taken from the manifestations of light, the hypothesis that the multiple luminosities correspond to small phenomena of consciousness is not, in my view, too far-fetched. If the luminosity should appear as monadic, as a single star for instance, or as an eye, then it easily takes on mandala formation and is then to be interpreted as the Self.[250]

I have gone into these analogous ideas at such length because I believe that Descartes's conception of the *lumen naturale* can be connected with these contemporary notions and is, in any case, based on a similar inner original experience. As Stephen Schönenberger points out in his article "A Dream of Descartes': Reflections on the Unconscious Determinants of the Sciences,"[251] alchemistic ideas often played a definite role in Descartes's thought,[252] although, for the most part, he misunderstood alchemical symbolism, taking it in a concretistic sense[253] and therefore rejecting it. As, in Paracelsus, the "natural light" also signifies human reason, so, according to Descartes, *"la raison"* consists of multiple *"semina scientiae"* ("seeds of science") or *"naturae simplices"* ("simple natures or beings") or *"veritates innatae"* ("inborn truths"). He also termed the ideas "primitive ideas" or "patterns, upon which we form all our other knowledge," ("notions primitives . . . originaux, sur le patron desquels nous formons nos autres connoissances"), but he reduced them to the conception of space, number, time, and one or two other elements.[254]

The image of the central sun was not lacking, either, in Descartes; in the *Regulae*[255] he says: "In their totality the sciences are nothing but human knowledge (*humana sapientia*), which ever remains one and the same, no matter how many objects are applied to it, just as the light of the sun is single among all the multiplicity of objects upon which it shines."[256] However, while these formulations shape the *intellectual working-out* of the original experience, it is the fiery sparks of the dream—as it were, its primal form or immediate, psychic manifestation—which, in their autonomy and reality beyond the scope of consciousness, terrify Descartes most profoundly.[257] These sparks are connected with the motif of the melon in the first part of the dream; for, as we have seen, the melon was considered by the Manichaeans to be a sort of "light-germ receptacle." This has now burst open, so to speak, and the luminosities appear directly before Descartes's eyes. In a certain sense the sparks occurring in the second dream correspond to the ghosts and the tempest in the first one, and, like the latter, they symbolize emotionally charged archetypal contents of the unconscious which were not contained in the framework of the church nor yet in Descartes's intellectual conception of the world.

Descartes shuts and opens his eyes until his fear and the phenomenon both vanish. He evidently tries to rationalize them away, just as he was altogether convinced that all so-called "miraculous" phenomena of nature could be rationally explained away.[258] This had a quieting effect, which is likewise evident in the atmosphere of the third dream, which is far less dramatic.

Interpretation of the Third Dream

In the third dream Descartes sees a book on the table but does not know who has placed it there; it is a dictionary, and he thinks that it will be very useful. But suddenly he finds that, instead of the dictionary, he is holding another book, without knowing where it has come from; it is a collection of poems, "*Corpus omnium veterum poetarum latinorum, etc.*, Lugduni, 1603,"[259] a book he had probably used at La Flèche.

The unmistakably magical way in which, throughout the

third dream, books appear on the table or disappear suggests the influence of ghosts and thus takes up the theme of the first dream;[260] but this time the ghosts play about with books but do not themselves appear. It seems to be the purpose of the unconscious to make clear to Descartes that, just as the creations of art are not "made" by consciousness, neither are the contents of all rational human knowledge (the dictionary undoubtedly stands for this); both *owe their existence to incalculable unconscious influences* and to their creative activities. In a certain sense, this is what Descartes tried to formulate in his *Cogito ergo sum,* in that for him the lucid awareness of one's own act of thinking, the immediate fact of oneself as a thinking being, in short, this consciousness of oneself, is that which guarantees not only the existence of one's own being but also that of God, inasmuch as God is the primal cause and source of all truth and of reality.[261] From this source come all those judgments which are irrefutably convincing to everybody, the sum total of which constitutes the *lumen naturale*[262] which originates in the *naturae purae et simplices* ("pure and simple natures")—the inborn ideas.[263] These latter he also compares with the *"tableaux ou images"* in the individual soul.[264] They are stored away *"in mentis thesauro"* ("in the treasury of the mind"),[265] from whence they must be lifted up. The "natural light" is the *res cogitans* in us;[266] it stems from God.[267] I consider it most probable that these fundamental premises of the Cartesian philosophy were born of the experience of the night of 10/11 November 1619—*that they represent, so to speak, the form in which Descartes endeavored to master, with his thinking, this incursion of the unconscious. But he only partially succeeded in doing justice to the contents of the unconscious* because he tried to grasp them with his thinking only (his superior function) and possibly with his intuition, and he did not consider the feeling and sensation side of his experience.[268] Besides, the irrational way in which the books are conjured up and then disappear—which cannot be explained causally[269]—contradicts his contention that the original substance of our thinking can only be clear and lucid and can only operate according to reason. Descartes was undoubtedly seriously concerned with the question of the illusion of reality, as experienced in dreams, and with the possibility that a cunning evil spirit lays "traps" for our thoughts, leading us astray into illusions and wrong conclusions;[270] but certain truths, above all the realization of oneself as a thinking subject, are somehow left out. The act of reflection—in its literal sense, the thought which bends back on itself—is for him the ultimate basis of reality of human existence and leads to the discovery of our consciousness of God,[271] which is set above man's existence and encompasses it. *But what the source of the illusions is, Descartes never investigated more closely;* no doubt in his opinion it is the *passiones animae* ("emotions")[272] and the sense perceptions which mislead people into wrong conclusions, but who or what engenders them he does not inquire. It is therefore significant, as Felsch notes,[273] that his application of the principle of causality is, especially in all psychological connections, dark and illogical. He projects the mystery of the connection between psyche and body onto the pineal gland,[274] which ostensibly rules the "spirits of life" in the ventricles of the brain. A continuous something must somehow exist between the *"res extensa"* and the *"res cogitans,"* but Descartes is unable to define it more closely.[275] The same lack of clarity prevails in regard to both his definition of imagination—which to him is a psychophysical event[276]—and the "passions of the soul" (*passiones*), which are allegedly brought about, now by the "spirits of life," now by the *"actio animae"* ("activity of the soul"), and then again by the impressions affecting the brain (*"impressiones quae casu occurrunt in cerebro"* ["impressions occurring in the brain by chance"]), or else by sensory objects.[277]

The unconscious inhibition that hindered Descartes from investigating this complex of problems more deeply must, in the final analysis, have been his adherence to the Christian definition of evil as a mere *privatio boni,*[278] a question that I would, in principle, refer to Jung's exposition in *Aion.*[279] In his *Cogitationes privatae*[280] Descartes says that God is *"intelligentia pura"* ("pure intelligence") and that, when He separated the light from the darkness, He separated the good from the evil angels. Since the *"privatio"* could not be separated from the *"habitus"* ("habitual behavior"), the darkness and the evil angels are only a *privatio* and its form of existence. As Sirven points out,[281] he is here quoting word for word from Saint Augustine's *De Genesi ad litteram liber imperfectus*[282] and *De Genesi contra Manichaeos*.[283] Just at the time of his dream, Descartes was himself considering the idea of writing a commentary on Genesis and had been reading these works of Augustine's.[284] We may assume that he took the *privatio boni* over from Saint Augustine[285] and half-unconsciously, as it were, blended it with his declaration that God is *"intelligentia pura"* and is thus absolutely veracious and unable to deceive.[286]

With this view Descartes remains ensnared in a Christian prejudice; it is as if the Trinitarian system should be applied to matter and cosmic reality but, again, without asking the question about the Fourth, the Totality. Maritain is therefore correct in saying that Descartes's philosophy appears with an *"air d'héroisme géomètre et chrétien"*—measuring the earth and straightway finding God in the soul.[287] He further emphasizes (see Gilson for supporting evidence) that Cartesian philosophy "breaks into two contrasing bits, which it asserts as separate existents never again capable of being reunited into those higher conciliations Scholasticism had made between the great antinomies of reality."[288] I believe this breaking-in-two of the Scholastic view of the world may be looked upon as a *doubling* of the same, in other words, as an unconscious realization of its "lower" correspondence. As Jung has explained,[289] the divine Trinity has its counterpart in a lower, chthonic triad[290] which "represents a principle which, by reason of its symbolism, betrays affinities with evil, though it is by no means certain that it expresses nothing but evil." This lower element has the relation of *correspondencia* ("correspondence") with the higher, but, in contradistinction to quaternary symbols, the triadic ones are not symbolic of wholeness. Jung continues: "If one imagines the quaternity as a square divided into two halves by a diagonal, one gets two triangles whose apices point in opposite directions. One could therefore say metaphorically that as the whole symbolized by the quaternity is divided into equal halves, it produces two opposing triads." The lower triangle represent a "dark spirit," which is indeed the cause of the present-day collective catastrophes but which, when rightly understood, can also become the *causa instrumentalis* of the process of individuation.[291] *This* spirit which seized Descartes is from the point of view of the Church a *malin génie* ("evil spirit"); but it is also a *spiritus familiaris* ("familiar spirit") that incites toward the achievement of wholeness. As Pauli explains in his article on Kepler, the latter's three-dimensional scheme of space is dependent on the Christian idea of the Trinity; and, similarly, Descartes's mechanistic, purely causal comprehension of nature, on the basis of the simple laws of movement, is founded on the Christian image of God. Thus it becomes evident that materialism, so-called, among whose founders Descartes must be numbered, really has its roots, as Brunschvicg remarks,[292] in an extreme form of spirituality. Thus, basically, Descartes completely "dematerialized" matter, in comparison with the way in which it is described in the newer physics, for, according to definition, he only concedes it a geometrically comprehensible dimension of space in three parameters, but not density, mass, or qualities of energy.[293] This connects up with the fact that he denied any movement of light taking place in time. He believed in an absolutely instantaneous spreading-out of light, a point against which Beeckmann, his contemporary, was already raising objections.[294] The uncritical acceptance of the definition of evil as a *privatio boni* and the identification of God's workings with logical, rational, causally explainable events made it impossible for him, in the sphere of his researches into natural science, to give further thought to an acausal description of occurrences. For this reason the unconscious emphasizes the reality of such phenomena in a compensatory manner and displays an autonomous ghostly effect.

Descartes's own association to the dictionary is that it represents the sum total of all the sciences (whose basic principle he believed he had just discovered mathematically); the collection of poems, on the other hand, stands for wisdom, enthusiasm, divine inspiration, and the seed of wisdom (which is to be found in the soul of man, as sparks in flint). However satisfying this thought may be at first sight, one cannot help being surprised that two poems by the Gallic poet Ausonius (fourth century A.D.) should represent this world of wisdom and inspiration; for the poems of this skeptical "poet," who wrote in a purely rhetorical style and merely went over to Christianity conventionally (!), contain, from our point of view, very little poetic inspiration. On the other hand, the two idylls which appear in the dream are both confessions of a possibly ingenious but purely skeptical *Weltanschauung*,[295] that of a man who is weary of life and even opposed to it. At first Descartes's eye falls on Idyll XV ("Ex Graeco Pythagoricum de ambiguitate eligendae vitae"), which begins with the words: "Quod vitae sectabor iter? Si *plena tumultu / sunt fora;* si curis domus anxia: si *peregrinos /* Cura domus sesequitur, . . ." These first lines fit Descartes's own situation in an amazing way—namely, that of the *peregrinus* ("stranger in the land, wanderer") in the very heart of Germany, then endangered by war. The poem then proceeds to state that neither work nor marriage nor riches, neither youth nor age, not even eternal life or mortality, can bring man happiness, and it ends with the words: "Optima Graiorum sententia: Quippe homini aiunt / non nasci esse bonum, natum aut cito morte potiri."[296]

In a certain sense, the question in the introductory sentence of the poem is on the same lines as the symbolism of the first dream, which showed that, "gripped" by the raging storm, Descartes was in danger of overlooking the rounding-out and maturing of his own personality. Here, also, the question calls his attention back, as it were, to the moral and personal problem[297] of his feeling, to the choice or decision in favor of the personal life. But here again another man appears, this time an unknown man, who draws his attention to yet another idyll. *This unknown person might be the figure of the "trickster,"*[298] *now become visible,* who spirited the books about in such an uncanny way. In any case, he represents an unknown, unconscious part of Descartes's personality, which might perhaps be a parallel to Mr. N. of the first dream, although Mr. N. was merely overlooked by Descartes, whereas this new arrival is completely unknown to him. The stranger recommends to him an idyll by Ausonius beginning "Est et Non" ("Yes and No").²⁹⁹ Idyll 12 = Ναὶ καὶ οὐ Πυθαγορικόν ("The Yes and No of the Pythagoreans").

The theme of the poem is that these two little words, "yes" and "no," govern all human life and set men at variance, and that everything can be affirmed and denied, so that many would prefer to remain completely silent. If the poem "Quod vitae sectabor iter" tried to awaken doubt and insecurity where the values of life are concerned, this last poem kindles doubt as to the reliability of all human statements; the "yes" and "no" are entirely relative. *The unknown man appears to be bent on undermining Descartes's belief in the possibility of absolutely valid proofs* and on convincing him of the paradoxical character of every really psychologically true statement—presumably with the intention of thus detaching him, as previously by means of the first poem, from his thinking function, which was growing more and more absolute, and of leading him toward the problem of his own self. At the same time the two poems *mirror Descartes's unconscious feeling attitude:*³⁰⁰ he has no faith at all in life and none in himself or in any other person. In his portraits one cannot help being struck by his hopelessly skeptical, timid, lifeless expression. It is without doubt the fact of his mother's early death which robbed him of any zest for life, of any faith in life and in his own feeling, so that he shut himself off in the sole activity of his mind. Also, it seems to me that his apparent lack of character is better explained as a certain deficiency of this sort of vital substance than as a flaw in his nature.

In the dream Descartes takes up the stranger's suggestion, appears to be quite *"au fait"* and wants to show the stranger the poem in his book but is unable to find it. The trickster's game starts anew; the stranger inquires where he got the book. He evidently wants to make it clear to Descartes—as we have already hinted—that all his sudden ideas and inspirations, his thinking and feeling, which he firmly believes to be under his control, being convinced that *he* is doing it all (*"Je pense donc je suis"*), are in reality entirely dependent on the good grace of the unconscious—on whether it chooses to supply them or not. This is why the dictionary appears again. But it is no longer complete: parts of it have crumbled away, since the problem of feeling has come up. Descartes then finds the idylls of Ausonius in the anthology, but not the poem "Est et Non," and he wants to recommend the other one ("Quod vitae sectabor") to the stranger instead. He tries to turn away from the problem of the doubtful nature of all thinking statements and, at the same time, to accept consciously his skeptical feeling side, which is inimical to life. But once again the unexpected happens: he finds small colored portraits, copper-plate engravings, which do not figure in the actual edition. The fact of touching the problem of feeling, the fourth function, has the effect of bringing up the idea of the individual personality[301] and of interest in the individual value and actual reality of each unique human being. This was just the period of the great Italian and Dutch portraitists, and this interest in individual personality corresponded to the tendency of the age. There is a multiplicity of portraits, which suggests an initial state of the as yet dissociated fragments of Descartes's personality. Like the many seeds of the melon, these are, as it were, the components inherited from the ancestors, out of which the "united personality" is gradually brought together.

In the first dream the symbol of the Self consists of a round object—the Monas. Emphasis is laid on unity. In the two following dreams, on the other hand, the new content of the Self is pictured as a plurality of sparks or portraits. It appears in multiple form, so to speak. This points to the fact that through the first meeting with the center, the Self (which is not the same as the ego), a duplication of the personality takes place. The unity of consciousness (and Descartes himself certainly saw the âme pensante, the thinking ego, as the only psychic reality) is cracked open. The dream shows that inwardly man is in reality manifold and inextricably bound up with the many. The ideal, connected with Christian monotheism, of the unity of consciousness and will, which was especially striven after by the Jesuits, is here called into question. For the Self, as Jung says, comprises not only the single man but also many others. "It is paradoxically the quintessence of the individual and at the same time a collectivity."[302]

Whereas Descartes's own dream interpretation is, on the whole, somewhat feeble and optimistic, in the final motif of the portraits it misses the mark altogether: he takes it to be a forecast of the visit of an Italian painter, who did in fact come to see him on the following day.[303] At least he sees that there might be a prophetic value, a *"valeur prophétique,"* in his dream and feels himself confirmed in seeing the operation of God in it. Therefore he says that, "the human mind had no part in it" ("l'esprit humain n'y avoit aucune part"). Although the incident was calculated to stress the importance of the portraits, Descartes does not appear to have grasped that they could be connected with his feeling side. The later development of his thought actually put more and more distance between himself and the "pictures." In his earlier writings and studies of the phenomenon of memory he granted a far higher value to the symbol of the pictures and to imagination, as "shadows" or images of a higher truth, as it were; but later he dissociated himself from these conceptions.[304] Perhaps this was the reason why the dream refers with such emotional intensity to just this particular aspect of the spirit. In this connection the visit of the painter on the following day should be looked upon as a synchronistic event, which intensified the significance of the dream. It is amazing how the statement about the *"valeur prophétique"* of the dream appeared to be a satisfactory "explanation" for Descartes, who normally dismissed the thought of an acausal connection of events. The implications of his remark seem to have eluded him. Subsequently, however, he did instinctively do something for his feeling side, which, in his case, was doubtless bound up with his dead mother: he vowed to go on a pilgrimage to the Madonna of Loretto, to pray for inner guidance in his *"recherche de la vérité,"* for after the dream he felt deep contrition as a sinner. His feeling of contrition (of being overwhelmed with regret) was caused in all probability by an illegitimate shifting of his feeling of inferiority onto certain sins of the past;[305] his real feeling of inferiority was doubtless based on the fact that the dream had touched the split-off problem of his feeling and the religious problem of evil.

What makes these dreams so impressive to me—quite apart from all they tell us about Descartes—is the fact that they already sketch, in a nutshell, the actual problem of the man of our time, the heir to that epoch of eighteenth-century rationalism, at the dawn of which Descartes stands, and, through the symbols of the melon and the individual portraits they point to the process of individuation as a possible lysis. Even though it is evident, not only from the conclusions which Descartes himself drew from the dreams but from the later trend of his life, that in some respects he failed to follow the way indicated by the unconscious, it is yet his merit to have worked with such passionate devotion for the "purification" of his mind and for the *"recherche de la vérité."*[306] This is undoubtedly the reason he was granted this important manifestation from the unconscious.

Conclusion

My interpretation of the dreams may seem rather critical and be felt to disparage Descartes's personality, but this is by no means my intention. My criticism is directed against Cartesian rationalism, which still influences man today. In other words, I have sought to demonstrate the inadequacy of a purely rational view of the world, which was a historically conditioned reaction against certain uncritical trends in medieval thought. From the opposing standpoint, Rittmeister has given more prominence to Descartes's merit in having established an ego-strength and an ego-freedom in his work, through which the development of modern science first became possible.[307] This is undoubtedly very much to the point. Today, however, the rationalism of science has become so rigidly established that it discards and even threatens to destroy feeling and with it our whole soul. It seems interesting, therefore, that already in Descartes's dream (which stood at the beginning of this recent development) this danger was symbolically indicated. The dream itself shows that the unconscious does not criticize the dreamer; he commits no offense in it, apart from failing to greet Mr. N. However, the unconscious does underline Descartes's relative lostness in an uncanny superpersonal situation which occurred as a result of his intense preoccupation with the problems of spiritual truth. He was certainly deeply touched and stirred by the dream-images, although his reasonable thinking extracted from them only a partial insight. But, looking at the symbolism with hindsight and from our modern standpoint, we can see how, through him, the archetype of the Self was seeking to become integrated, not only in his new thinking but in his human being as a whole, a task which still awaits the scientist of today.

Notes

1. In his *La Vie de M. Descartes* (2 vols., 1691), vol. 1, pp. 39 ff., 50–51; reprinted in C. Adam and P. Tannery, *Oeuvres de Descartes,* vol. 10, pp. 179ff. (hereafter cited as *"A-T."* The Adam and Tannery edition of the works of Descartes, published in Paris between 1897 and 1913 in twelve volumes and a supplement, superseded all others.) A German translation of Baillet's account of the dream appears in I. Ježower, *Das Buch der Träume* (Berlin, 1928), and it is Ježower's translation with which I have chiefly worked.

2. Jacques Maritain, *Le Songe de Descartes* (Paris: Corrêa, 1932), p. 292; English trans. M. L. Andison, *The Dream of Descartes, and Other Essays* (New York, 1944). See also Freud's letter to Maxim Leroy in Freud, *Gesammelte Schriften* (Vienna, 1934), vol. 12, pp. 403ff., English translation, "Some Dreams of Descartes: A Letter to Maxim Leroy," in *The Complete Psychological Works of Sigmund Freud,* ed. James Strachey et al. (London, 1927–31), vol. 21, pp. 203–204. Leroy's book *Descartes, le Philosophe au masque* was unfortunately not available to me. See also Heinrich Quiring, "Der Traum des Descartes," *Kant-Studien, Philosophische Zeitschrift* 46, no. 2 (1954–1955): 135f. Quiring considers the dream to be merely a consciously formed presentation in cipher of Descartes's theory of cosmogonic vortices. On the other hand, a professional psychologist must object that, throughout, the dream is genuine enough, exhibiting typical motifs that cannot have been invented.

3. I am indebted to E. A. Bennet, M.D., and F. Beyme, M.D., for calling my attention to these articles, which are difficult to find. Dr. Bennet was kind enough to get them for me.

4. *Confinia psychiatrica*, 4, no. 4 (1961): 65–98.

5. Cf. S. Gagnebin, "La réforme cartésienne et son fondement géometrique," *Gesnerus* (a quarterly published by the Schweizer Gesellschaft für Geschichte der Medizin und der Naturwissenschaften) 7, Fasc. 1 / 2 (1950): 119: "A la réflexion on en viendrait . . . à conclure que ce qui reste vivant du cartésianisme *c'est l'analogie de notre situation actuelle et de celle dans laquelle il s'est formé*. . . . La chose la plus curieuse c'est que, peut-être, la géométrie sera de nouveau au centre de la nouvelle réforme. C'est une géométrie qui est à la base de la Relativité généralisée." ("Upon reflection one would . . . reach the conclusion that that which remains living of Cartesian philosophy is the analogy of our present situation to that in which it was formed. . . . The most curious aspect is that geometry will, perhaps, once again be at the center of the new reform. It is geometry which is at the basis of generalized relativity.")

6. For the recent literature on Descartes, see G. Sebba, *Bibliographia cartesiana: A Critical Guide to the Descartes Literature, 1800–1960*, "Archives Internat. de l'Histoire des Idées," vol. 5 (The Hague: Nijhoff, 1964). See also Wolfgang Röd, *Descartes: Die innere Genesis des cartesianischen Systems* (Munich and Basel: Reinhardt, 1964), and the literature there cited.

7. Originally "de Quartis." Later Descartes's father took the title "gentilhomme de Poitou." His family belonged to the *petite noblesse*. His grandfather and one great-grandfather had been doctors.

8. For further details see C. Adam, *Descartes, sa vie et ses oeuvres* (Paris, 1910), p. 9 (hereafter cited as "Adam"; this work is vol. 12 of *A-T*). The eldest son, Pierre, had also died, so that only three children survived (ibid., p. 9).

9. Ibid., p. 15.

10. Ibid., p. 20.

11. Ibid., p. 7. He once said of his son that "il n'était bon qu'à se faire relier en veau" ("he was good for nothing but to be bound in calfskin") (ibid., p. 7 n.).

12. He once remarked: "Une belle femme se rencontre trop rarement, aussi rarement qu'un bon livre et un parfait prédicateur." ("A beautiful woman is met with all too seldom, as seldom as a good book or a perfect preacher.") (Ibid., p. 70.)
13. For further details see ibid., p. 41.
14. *A-T,* vol. 10, p. 52. Cf. also Etienne Gilson, "L'innéisme cartésien et la théologie," *Revue de métaphysique et de morale* 22 (1914): 465.
15. See Adam, pp. 47, 49; for further details see *A-T,* vol. 10, p. 252.
16. *A-T,* vol. 10, p. 193: "M. Descartes . . . se sentit ébranlé."
17. See, further, Maritain, pp. 13ff., and *A-T* vol. 10, pp. 193ff. However, he formed the initials R.C. in his seal, in exactly the same way as the Rosicrucians formed theirs (*A-T,* vol. 10, p. 48).
18. *A-T,* vol. 10, p. 63. In *Discours de la méthode* (*A-T,* vol. 6, p. 9) he says: "Et enfin pour les mauvaises doctrines je pensois desia connoitre assés ce qu'elles valoient pour n'estre plus suiet a estre trompé, ny par les promesses d'un Alchemiste, ny par les prédictions d'un Astrologue, ny par les impostures d'un Magicien, ny par les artifices ou la vanterie d'aucun de ceux qui font profession de sçavoir plus qu'ils sçavent." ("And as for the false doctrines, I thought I already knew enough of their worth not to be liable to be deceived any more, whether by the promises of an Alchemist, or by the predictions of an Astrologer, or by the impostures of a Magician, or by the artifices or boastings of any of those who profess to know more than they do.") For details see J. Sirven, *Les Années d'apprentissage de Descartes (1596–1628)* (Paris, 1925), pp. 50–51, and the literature cited there.
19. Adam, p. 31.
20. *A-T,* vol. 10, p. 6.
21. Sirven, pp. 51, 113, and nn.
22. Ibid., p. 69. (*Democritica* has been lost.) Descartes also occupied himself with the meaning of his dream and its "divine character" (ibid., p. 69; see also *A-T,* vol. 11, p. 468).
23. Concerning his attitude toward the Virgin see Adam, p. 27.

24. Cf. Cay von Brockdorff, *Descartes und die Fortbildung der Kartesischen Lehre* (Munich, 1923), pp. 15ff., and Adam, pp. 64ff., 73, and 95.
25. The latter painted his portrait. Cf. Adam, p. 101.
26. Letter to Plempius (*A-T,* vol. 1, p. 527). He believed that animals were automata (cf. Sirven, p. 321).
27. Adam, pp. 161, 193, and 233. He also had an experimental botanical garden (ibid., p. 495).
28. For details see von Brockdorff, p. 16. Cf. also Gagnebin, p. 109, or Descartes's letter of December 1640, to Mersenne (*A-T,* vol. 3, p. 263ff. and 394ff.) Concerning his alleged insincerity and cowardice see Maritain, pp. 50–52.
29. Regarding Descartes's theory of the whirlwind, cf. J. O. Fleckenstein, "Cartesische Erkenntnis und mathematische Physik des 17. Jahrhunderts," *Gesnerus* 7, nos. 3–4 (1950): 120ff.: "From out of the small spheres of the four basic elements arise vortices that lead to the formation of the world."
30. Von Brockdorff, pp. 24ff., and Adam, pp. 331, 341, and 366.
31. Von Brockdorff, pp. 19–21.
32. Adam, pp. 230ff., 287; also p. 575n: "La mort de Francine lui causa 'le plus grand regret, qu'il eût jamais senti de sa vie.' " ("Francine's death caused him 'the most regret he had ever felt in his life.' ") Cf. also pp. 337ff.
33. Adam, p. 16. Many biographies make much ado about his duel on account of a lady during his student days. But this event strikes me as a purely social affair, with no deeper significance.
34. Ibid., pp. 512ff.
35. Ibid., p. 549.
36. Ibid., p. 49.
37. For this period of his life, see Sirven's standard work (*Les Années d'apprentissage*) and the literature there cited, especially pp. 141n and 152.
38. Vol. 1, pp. 39ff. and 50–51. See note 1, above.
39. "X Novembris 1619 cum plenus forem Enthousiasmo et mirabilis scientiae fundamenta reperirem, . . ." (*A-T,* vol. 10, p. 179).
40. "XI Novembris 1620 coepi intelligere fundamentrum Inventi mirabilis" (ibid.).

41. Cf. Sirven, p. 122.
42. He explained "lying long in bed" as *"tristitia,"* and in the
    Cogitationes privatae (A-T, vol. 10, p. 215) he says: "Adverto
    me, si tristis sim, aut in periculo verser, et tristia occupent
    negotia, altum dormire et comedere avidissime; si vero
    laetitia distendar, nec edo nec dormio." ("I notice that if I
    am sad, or thrown in danger, and sad affairs take up my
    time, I sleep deeply and eat greedily, but if joy fills me, I
    neither eat nor sleep.")
43. Sirven, p. 114.
44. "Après que j'eus employé quelques années à étudier ainsi
    dans le livre du monde et à tâcher d'acquérir quelque
    expérience, je pris un jour résolution d'étudier *aussi en moi-
    même* et d'employer toutes les forces de mon esprit à choisir
    les chemins que je davais suivre; ce qui me réussit beaucoup
    mieux, ce me semble, que si je ne me fusse jamais éloigné
    ni de mon pays, ni de mes livres."
45. *A-T,* vol. 6, pp. 16–17. Cf. also Sirven, p. 115.
46. "Mais comme un homme qui marche seul et dans les
    ténèbres, je me résolus d'aller si lentement et d'user tant de
    circonspection en toutes choses, que si je n'avais que fort
    peu, je me gardais bien, au moins de tomber."
47. In contradistinction to Sirven (p. 116), I consider that
    Maritain is absolutely correct in comparing this exercise of
    Descartes's with the *via purgativa* of the mystics, though it
    is, indeed, actually displaced onto an intellectual plane.
48. *A-T,* vol. 10, p. 189.
49. Cf. Sirven, pp. 121, 298. Unfortunately Gustave Cohen's
    work *Ecrivains français en Hollande de la première moitié du
    XVIIᵉ siècle* (Paris, 1920) was not available to me.
50. For further details see Adam, p. 50, and Sirven, passim.
51. Optics and mechanics were subsequently added.
52. *Regulae (A-T,* vol. 10, p. 451): ". . . sciendum est omnes
    habitudines quae inter entia eiusdem generis esse possunt,
    ad duo capita esse referendas: nempe ad ordinem, vel ad
    mensuram." (". . . it is necessary to know that all relations
    that can exist among existents of this kind are drawn up
    under two headings: namely, hierarchical order and meas-
    urable proportion.") Concerning the importance of this
    experience cf. also Léon Brunschvicg, *Descartes et Pascal:
    Lecteurs de Montaigne* (Neuchâtel, 1945), pp. 102 ff.

53. Adam, p. 55.
54. G. Milhaud, *Descartes savant* (Paris, 1921), cited in Maritain, p. 255.
55. H. Poincaré, "Die mathematische Erfindung," in *Wissenschaft und Methode* (Leipzig and Berlin, 1914), pp. 35ff.
56. Quoted ibid., p. 38.
57. Ibid., p. 39.
58. Ibid., pp. 41–42.
59. Ibid., pp. 44–45.
60. Ibid., pp. 47, 48.
61. Princeton, 1949. Cf. B. L. van der Waerden, *Einfall und Überlegung: Drei kleine Beiträge zur Psychologie des mathematischen Denkens* (Basel and Stuttgart: Birkhäuser, 1954).
62. P. 17 and passim.
63. In his edition of Descartes's *Discours de la méthode: texte et commentaire* (Paris, 1947), pp. 60, 157, and 214, cited in Sirven, pp. 123–124 and 167.
64. My note: In *Le Songe* . . . Maritain also admits this, but he stresses that Descartes really believed that one man could reform science and that he was that man.
65. ". . . everything that is capable of being truly understood is . . . by definition capable of being known mathematically. The idea of the unity of the body of the sciences . . . is therefore inseparable, chronologically and logically, from the extension of the mathematical method to the totality of the domain of knowledge."
    Among other things Descartes also said, "Ces longues chaînes de raisons toutes simples et faciles dont les géomètres ont coutume de se servir . . . m'avaient donné occasion de m'imaginer que toutes les choses qui peuvent tomber sous la connaissance des hommes s'entresuivent en même façon." ("These long chains of reasons, all simple and easy, which geometers are in the habit of using . . . caused me to imagine that everything men can learn could be connected in the same way.") Quoted by J. Laporte, *Le Rationalisme de Descartes* (Paris, 1945), p. 13.
66. For examples see Laporte, p. 7n. The concepts of dimension, time, and space are for him the constituent concepts of pure knowledge; they are beyond questioning, whether seen waking or in a dream: "Atqui Arithmeticam, Geometricam . . . quae nonnisi de simplicissimis et maxime

generalibus rebus tractant, atque utrum eae sint in rerum natura necne parum curant aliquid certi atque indubitati continere. Nam sive vigilem, sive dormiam duo et tria simul iuncta sunt quinque, . . ." ("But arithmetic, geometry . . . deal only with the most simple and general things, and even if they appear in physical nature there is always something free from doubt and certain in them. For awake or asleep, two plus three is five.") (*A-T,* vol. 7, p. 20, quoted from H. Barth, "Descartes' Begründung der Erkenntnis" [diss., Bern, 1913], p. 33.) Concerning this question cf. also Prof. F. Gonseth, *Les mathématiques et la réalité* (Paris: Alcan, 1936), pp. 55ff.

67. Gonseth, pp. 58ff.; cf. also pp. 79ff., 376ff.

68. In a letter from Professor Gonseth to the author: "Les mathématiques se situent dans un champ de connaissance placé entre deux pôles complémentaires, l'un étant le monde des réalités dites extérieures, l'autre le monde des réalités dites intérieures. Ces deux mondes sont tous les deux transconscientiels. Ils ne sont ni l'un ni l'autra donnés tels quels, mais seulement par leur traces dans le champ conscientiel. Les mathématiques portent cette double trace." ("Mathematics is placed in a field of knowledge between two complementary poles: one the world of reality called exterior, the other, interior. These two worlds are beyond consciousness. They are not graspable as such, but their imprints appear in the field of consciousness. Mathematics shows this double imprint.")

69. Cf. the criticism of this view of Descartes's, that matter and consciousness are static objective *"entia,"* in A. N. Whitehead, *Science and the Modern World* (New York, 1948), pp. 201ff. Whitehead gives a generally readable sketch of Descartes's ideas and their development.

70. He says of arithmetic and geometry: "Haec enim prima rationis humanae continere et ad veritates ex quovis subiecto eliciendas se extendere debet." ("For this ought to contain the first [things] of human reason and be extended to the truths to be sought from any subject whatsoever.") (*A-T,* vol. 10, pp. 374–377, cited in Barth, p. 9). On the other hand, he gave up the play of purely numerical symbolism (see Barth).

71. Concerning this idea see C. G. Jung, "Synchronicity: An

Acausal Connecting Principle," *The Structure and Dynamics of the Psyche (CW 8)*.

72. Cf. also Sirven's explanation that he had found "les fondements consistant une méthode générale" ("the foundations composing a general method") (Sirven, pp. 126–27).
73. For an overall view, cf. E.-W. Platzeck, *Raimund Lull, sein Leben—seine Werke: Die Grundlagen seines Denkens*, 2 vols. (Düsseldorf: Schwann, 1962).
74. Cf. Jung, *The Archetypes and the Collective Unconscious (CW 9, Part I)*, and *Psychology and Alchemy (CW 12)*, passim.
75. Cf. Paolo Rossi, *Clavis Universalis: Arte mnemoniche e logica combinatoria da Lullio a Leibniz* (Milan, 1960), p. 48.
76. Cf. Frances Yates, *Giordano Bruno and the Hermetic Tradition* (London: Routledge & Kegan Paul, 1964).
77. Cf. Rossi, passim.
78. Milhaud, p. 56, cited in Sirven, pp. 55–57.
79. Sirven (p. 151) says, "Ses diverses remarques nous permettent d'expliquer sans peine comment Descartes est passé des 'spirtualia' aux 'Olympica,' des choses de l'esprit aux choses de Dieu. Il est parti du symbolisme mathématique pour former *un symbolisme intellectuel* et s'en est tenu d'abord aux exemples du vent et de la lumière, que lui avait légués la tradition scolaire. Mais la lecture de St. Augustin lui permit de passer aux choses divines et d'exprimer par de nouveaux exemples l'action de Dieu dans le monde." ("These miscellaneous remarks [i.e., Descartes's interpretation of the storm as spirit, etc.] allow us to explain quite easily Descartes's departure from 'spiritual things' to 'Olympica'; from the things of the spirit to the things of God. He left mathematical symbolism to form *an intellectual symbolism* and, at first, stuck to examples bequeathed him by school tradition. But study of Saint Augustine allows him to proceed to divine things and to express God's action in the world by means of new examples.")
80. Notice the expression *arte mirabili*.
81. Cf. Sirven, pp. 279, 298. The title of a publication in my possession runs as follows: *Ansa inauditae et mirabilis novae Artis Arcanis aliquot propheticis et Biblicis numeris . . . qua ordo semper a Deo observatus, dum numeris . . . Pyramidalibus observatus est . . .* (Frankfort, 1613). It deals chiefly with speculations concerning numbers mentioned in the Bible.

82. Cf. *Cogitationes privatae* (A-T, vol. 10, p. 215): "Larvatae nunc scientiae sunt quae, larvis sublatis, pulcherrime apparerent. *Catenam scientiarum pervidenti, non difficilius videbitur, eas animo retinere quam seriem numerorum.*" ("Now the disciplines are masked: these would appear most beautiful if the masks were removed. For anyone contemplating the chain, it seems no more difficult to remember them than the series of integers.") Cf. Sirven, pp. 226–27.

83. Sirven (pp. 123–24) is correct in drawing attention to *"reperirem"* (imperfect), meaning that he was only on the point of finding the *"scientia mirabilis"* and did not, therefore, already possess it. See also *A-T,* vol. 10, p. 360, First rule: "Scientiae omnes nihil aliud sunt quam humana sapientia quae una et eadem manet quantumvis differentibus subiectis applicata." ("All disciplines are nothing but human wisdom, always one and the same thing, applied to as many different subjects as you like.")

84. In general my rendering of Baillet follows I. Ježower's German translation in his *Das Buch der Träume,* pp. 90ff. I have nevertheless changed a few words ("college" instead of "seminary," "exotic" instead of "strange," and "bend down" in place of "throw down") in order to remain closer to the French text. I have put certain words in italics which are important in the ensuing interpretation.

85. Ježower translates *se renverser* as "throw down," but in that case Descartes would not have been able to go any farther.

86. It is fairly certain that he must have read this book at La Flèche. Cf. Adam, p. 21, n. 2.

87. Ježower: "was not so complete."

88. The same thought appears in the *Cogitationes privatae (A-T,* vol. 10, p. 217): "Mirum videri possit, quare graves sententiae in scriptis poetarum, magis quam philosophorum. Ratio est quod poetae per enthusiasmum et vim imaginationis scripsere: sunt in nobis semina scientiae, ut in silice, quae per rationem a philosophis educuntur per imaginationem a poetis excutiuntur magisque elucent." ("Wonderfully, poets abound more in serious thoughts than philosophers do. Poets write by force of imagination and with enthusiasm; all of us bear the seeds of wisdom within us, like flint, which are brought forth by the philosophers by reason, [but] the poets strike them forth with imagination, and they shine all the more brightly.")

89. Since the appearance of Milhaud's paper in the *Revue de métaphysique et de morale* (July 1916), pp. 610–11, it has been customary to look on the "Enthusiasmus" as coinciding with the dream, but I see no reason why Baillet's report should be depreciated; the dream appears to be far more a representation of the "meaning" of the enthusiasm.

90. Cf. C. G. Jung, "The Phenomenology of the Spirit in Fairy Tales," *The Archetypes and the Collective Unconscious*, pp. 212–13.

91. Ibid., pp. 208–209.

92. Cited by Jung, ibid., pp. 212–213.

93. Ibid., pp. 212–214. Descartes also hoped that science would make us "the masters and possessors of nature" (Adam, p. 229).

94. *A-T,* vol. 7, p. 27.

95. Barth, "Descartes' Begründung der Erkenntnis," p. 56.

96. The soul is the *"res cogitans"* (Barth, p. 59). See also Barth's comment (p. 53) on the following passage from Descartes's letter to Mersenne (*A-T,* vol. 3, p. 394): "Pour ce qui est de l'Ame, c'est encore une chose plus claire. Car n'étant comme j'ai démontré qu'une chose qui pense, il est impossible que nous puissions jamais penser à une chose que nous n'ayons en même temps l'idée de notre âme, comme d'une chose capable de penser à tout ce que nous pensons. . . ." ("Concerning the soul, it is something even more intelligible. For being, as I have demonstrated, nothing but a thing that thinks, it is impossible that we should ever think of something without at the same time having the idea of our soul, as of a thing capable of thinking of all that we think about.") It is also indicative of Descartes's type that he relegated feeling to the sphere of the body (see below, p. 87, n. 126).

97. Cf. Jung, *Psychological Types* (*CW* 6), chapter on definitions.

98. His main psychological function was probably introverted thinking. Cf. Fleckenstein's remark (p. 133): "To be sure, the portrayal of all the physical processes thus remains nothing but an image, a model, with which calculations can be undertaken."

99. Cf. Gonseth, p. 378: "Aussitôt qu'elles ont trouvé leur expression *les pensées revêtent une certaine existence autonome*.

L'esprit qui les a conçues les reconnaît comme siennes, mais ne les habite plus complètement." ("As soon as they have found their expression, thoughts take on a certain autonomy of existence. The mind that conceived them recognizes them as its own, but no longer inhabits them completely.") The ego is thus only a channel for intellectual contents which announce themselves preconsciously and, after their formulation, autonomously pursue their further development.

100. Quite correctly Maritain speaks, concerning Descartes, of a "mythe de la science." (Cf. Sirven, p. 308n.)

101. Jung says this concerning Paracelsus; see his *Paracelsica* (Zurich, 1942), p. 45. Henri Bergson has also correctly described Descartes's mathematics and *"méthode"* as a *"proles sine matre creata"* ("offspring created without a mother"). (See Sirven [p. 1], who follows H. Bergson, "La Philosophie," *Science française* [Paris, 1916]).

102. In the *Cogitationes privatae (A-T,* vol. 10, p. 214), he says: "Scientia est velut mulier, quae si pudica apud virum maneat, colitur; si communis fiat, vilescit." ("Science is like a woman, who is cherished if she remains modest with one man, but becomes cheap if she prostitutes herself to many.")

103. Descartes knew the work of "Vitellio" (Witelo) and Kepler's "Paralipomena ad Vitellionem," as well as Galileo's works (see Sirven, p. 283).

104. "Die Einfluss archetypischer Vorstellungen auf die Bildung naturwissenschaftlicher Theorien bei Kepler," in C. G. Jung and W. Pauli, *Naturerklärung und Psyche* (Zurich: Rascher Verlag, 1952); English trans. by Priscilla Silz, "The Influence of Archetypal Ideas on the Scientific Theories of Kepler," in C. G. Jung and W. Pauli, *The Interpretation of Nature and the Psyche* (New York and London, 1955).

Professor Pauli had the kindness to send me the following explanations by letter: "There has also been an attempt in principle to take the psychic conditioning factors of the observer into account. Kepler also does this, but with the tendency, ever more apparent, to eliminate them from the 'objective' observation of nature."

105. Cf. *Meditation* 4: "I believe that that whole class of causes

that one is in the habit of inferring from their ends should not be used in physics" (cited in Carl Felsch, *Der Kausalitätsbegriff bei Descartes* [Langensalza, 1891], p. 11).

106. In his letter, cited above, n. 104, Pauli says: "Concerning the modern 'anima-problem,' [we may remember that] the seventeenth century tried to *eliminate the concept of soul from the physical world.* The tendency was therefore to limit the soul more and more to the individual human being. What was abandoned . . . was the idea of the objective-psychic factor. In the seventeenth century the psyche became purely subjective."

107. This lack of the conception of the *anima mundi* in Descartes's view of the physical world is consequently also to be connected with his personal problem of not being able to integrate his personal anima.

108. *Meditation* 6 and *Principia* 2.36–37. Cf. Hyman Stock, *The Method of Descartes in the Natural Sciences* (New York, 1931), pp. 11–15.

109. *Principia* 2.23; cf. also Stock, p. 12.

110. Stock, p. 11.

111. Stock, p. 12, commenting on *Meditation* 6.

112. Barth, p. 87.

113. Cf. Felsch, *Der Kausalitätsbegriff bei Descartes,* p. 9.

114. Ibid., pp. 9–10.

115. Röd, *Descartes: Die innere Genesis des cartesianischen Systems,* passim.

116. Felsch, p. 8.

117. Ibid., p. 9.

118. *Principia phil.,* 1. 39, 49, 75, cited in Felsch, p. 14.

119. Felsch, p. 15.

120. As Fleckenstein (p. 135) stresses: "Descartes was unable to conceive of the mathematical formulation of continuous functions because he tended to eliminate the parameter of time in physics. It was Newton who introduced the time-parameter into physics, and in his private thoughts on metaphysics he even called it a substance of the '*vita divina*'—just as for him space was the '*sensorium Dei.*' " Fleckenstein also remarks (p. 126): "The basis of Cartesian mechanics is the conservation of the impulse or, in its original form, of the quantum of movement which is the product of mass and velocity. Descartes did not yet know

of the vectorial aspect of velocity and saw it only as a scalar factor, which led him into contradictions when deriving his laws of impulse. . . . Since Descartes only used the laws of analytical geometry within the framework of Euclidean geometry, he overcame the prejudices of the physics of antiquity in form but not in essence, for his mechanics remain identical with those of antiquity." Ibid., p. 127: "In the world of Descartes there are only rigid collisions which transfer the quantum of movement, but not continually acting forces causing changes of state. He tried to understand cosmic events from the multiplicity of distribution of the movement-quantum instead of understanding it from what remains continuous within the temporal changes. It was Leibniz who later achieved this by his principle of energy, which he had to defend in his dispute with the Cartesians." Ibid., p. 128: "Descartes is unable to grasp a continuous change, especially not in time, for he aims at an elimination of the time-parameter in his 'geometrization' of physics." Cf. also ibid., pp. 123 ff.

121. "Synchronicity: An Acausal Connecting Principle," (*CW* 8).

122. Naturally Descartes could not recognize the principle of synchronicity in the Jungian sense, but he discarded its earlier manifestations, such as the doctrine of correspondences, the *causa finalis,* and so forth.

123. Concerning whom see von Brockdorff, p. 152.

124. Professor Pauli has drawn attention to these facts.

125. Cf. von Brockdorff, pp. 19 ff.

126. He puzzled over the function of the pineal gland, which he conjectured to be the "connecting place" of body and soul. For details of this particular problem see Geoffrey Jefferson, "René Descartes on the Localisation of the Soul," *Irish Journal of Medical Science,* no. 285 (September 1949), pp. i ff., and the literature cited there. I am indebted to Dr. E. A. Bennet for drawing my attention to this article.

127. In his paper, "Three Dreams of Descartes," *International Journal of Psycho-Analysis* 28, pt. 1 (1947): 11ff., J. O. Wisdom interprets this motif as Descartes's unconscious fear of impotence (castration complex), though, unless one is inclined to believe in the Freudian theory of the "censor," it is baffling to know why Descartes should suffer

from such a fear or why it should be depicted in such a form. No specifically sexual disturbances are perceptible in Descartes's case, but rather an atrophying of the life of feeling. On the other hand, Wisdom (28ff.) rightly stresses the conflict in Descartes between his intellect and his urge for life. I wish to thank the author for sending me his article.

128. *"Se renverser."*

129. Cf. J. Rittmeister, "Die mystische Krise des jungen Descartes," *Confinia psychiatrica* 4 (1961): 81, where the "left" is interpreted similarly to the way in which I have sought to work it out. The "left side" corresponds to the dark side of the inferior function, which in intellectual types is usually feeling. For Descartes it becomes the devil, who reverses the previous point of view and (in the case of the dreamer) lames him in the feet. Does it not, says Rittmeister, in fact strike us that the longing for the mother, the home, and so forth applies to all those mythological characters, such as Harpocrates (Horus), Hephaestus, Oedipus, the Philoctetes, who were crippled in their lower limbs? Concerning the left side as feminine and chthonic see Bachofen, *Versuch über die Gräbersymbolik der Alten* (Basel, 1859), pp. 171ff.: "The left hand of Isis, *aequitatis manus,* is one of the symbols carried around in the procession." Apuleius *Metamorphoses* XI and 1: "The left hand is 'otiosa.' " Macrobius *Sat.* 7.13: "Boys are begotten from the right testicle, girls from the left one." See also Plutarch *Symp.* 8.8. and 5.7. According to Plato (*Laws* 4) the left side and an even number of sacrificial animals were offered to the chthonic gods, while the Olympians received the right side and an uneven number. The left is associated with the North, the right with the South. Sacrifices to or for the dead are performed with the left hand. Cf. Jung, *Psychology and Alchemy,* p. 121, concerning the circumambulation to the left: "The left, the 'sinister' side, is the unconscious side. Therefore a leftward movement is equivalent to a movement in the direction of the unconscious, whereas a movement to the right is 'correct' and aims at consciousness." Cf. also Jung's commentary on dream 22 in the same volume (p. 156), where "The 'left' is to be completely throttled" and where Jung further re-

marks (pp. 160–61, 163–65): "Just as the 'right' denotes the world of consciousness and its principles, so by 'reflection' the picture of the world is to be turned round to the left, thus producing a corresponding world in reverse. We could equally well say: through reflection the right appears as the reverse of the left. Therefore the left seems to have as much validity as the right; in other words, the unconscious and its—for the most part unintelligible—order becomes the symmetrical counterpart of the conscious mind and its contents, although it is still not clear which of them is reflected and which reflecting. To carry our reasoning a step further, we could regard the center as the point of intersection of two worlds that correspond but are inverted by reflection."

130. In *The Structure and Dynamics of the Psyche* (*CW* 8).

131. In the *Cogitationes privatae* (*A-T*, vol. 10, p. 218), Descartes himself says that the wind is the spirit: "Ventus spiritum designat, motus cum tempore vitam, lumen cognitionem, calor amorem, activitas instantanea creationem." ("Wind designates spirit; movement with time: life; light: cognition; heat: love; instantaneous activity: creation.")

132. Rittmeister (pp. 81–82) thinks that the direction of the storm is a regression into the primordial past and to the Mother of God.

133. See *A-T*, X, 18 ff.

134. Friedrich Nietzsche, *Thus Spoke Zarathustra,* end of chapter 28, "The Rabble" (New York: Modern Library), p. 111. J. O. Wisdom interprets the wind as the father-image, which appears to be both fertilizing and threatening, when Descartes attempts to consummate the sexual act (Wisdom, pp. 15–16).

135. Maritain (p. 25) stresses the extent to which Descartes felt himself to have been possessed by a kind of "*Sapientia Dei*" or by the Holy Ghost: "C'est ainsi, croyons nous, que Descartes aperçut, ramassée dans une seule intuition, l'idée vitale, le Λόγος σπερματικός ["seminal Word"] de sa réforme philosophique." ("It was thus, so we believe, that Descartes perceived and gathered together into one single intuition the vital idea, the *Logos spermatikos* of his philosophical reform.") He believed (cited in Maritain, p. 25) ". . . à la Science universelle qui élèvera notre nature à son

plus haut degré de perfection" (". . . in the universal science which will elevate our nature to its highest degree of perfection"). Maritain continues (p. 27): "L'enthousiasme solitaire qui l'anime a une origine divine, l'ivresse de la nuit du 10 novembre 1619 est une ivresse sainte, elle est en sa personne comme une pentecôte de la raison." ("The lonely enthusiasm that animates him has a divine origin; the intoxication of the night of 10 November 1619 is a holy drunkenness; in itself it is like a Pentecost of reason.") (P. 30): "[C'est] la science même de Dieu et des Anges. S'il en est ainsi, c'est sans doute par un effet de l'idéalisme et si j'ose dire de l'angélisme qui caractérise en général la philosophie cartésienne." ("It is the very science of God and the angels. If it be thus, it is without doubt as a consequence of the idealism, or, if I may say, the angelic quality, which in general characterizes Cartesian philosophy.") Maritain (p. 31) understands very clearly the *hubris* of the new scientific thinking and for that reason believes that "c'est le songe d'une nuit d'automne *excité par un malin génie* dans un cerveau de philosophe . . ." (". . . it is the dream of an autumn night, *instigated in the brain of a philosopher by a malicious spirit* . . .").

136. Concerning the idea that behind this outbreak of the German spirit stands the image of Wotan cf. Jung, "Wotan" (*CW* 10), esp. pp. 16ff. Wotan (Odin) is a wind- or storm-god, the leader of the *wüetis heer,* i.e., the host of the dead, the great magician who, as Jung says (ibid.), embodies ". . . the impulsive emotional, as well as the intuitive and inspirational side of the unconscious." For the mythological phenomenology see Martin Ninck, *Wodan und germanischer Schicksalsglaube* (Jena, 1935), and E. Mogk, *Germanische Religionsgeschichte und Mythologie* (Berlin and Leipzig: Gruyter, 1927), pp. 64ff. Wotan also behaves like a ghost-figure (ibid., p. 65). He is the first engenderer of enthusiasm (ibid., p. 67); he is also a deluder of women (ibid., p. 74) and a magician.

137. According to Fleckenstein, pp. 122–24.

138. Ibid.

139. Cf. Jung, *Psychology and Alchemy,* p.23.

140. My note: Cf. the chapter on "Definitions" in Jung's *Psychological Types.*

141. Cf. *Psychology and Alchemy,* pp. 101–104, 119–120, and esp. 144, 148, and 153.
142. Thus does Maritain conclude his paper "Le Songe . . ." (pp. 5–7). Unfortunately he considers that to Catholics "le commerce avec les génies excitateurs des songes" ("traffic with spirits instigating dreams") can only seem suspect.
143. *A-T,* vol. 10, p. 185.
144. Ibid.
145. Cf. the following articles in *Patr. Lat.* (ed. Migne): "Rhabanus Maurus," vol. 110, col. 860; "Adam Scotus," vol. 198, col. 760; "St. Eucharist.," vol. 50, col. 739; "St. Victor Garnerius," vol. 193, col. 59; "Gregor Magnus," vol. 76, cols. 1019, 1026, and 1054; etc. Further details in Jung, *Aion (CW 9,* part I).
146. See Philipp Funk, *Ignatius von Loyola* (Berlin, 1913), pp. 57, 66. Cf., further, Jung's exposition in "The Process of Individuation" (Eidgenössische Technische Hochschule Lectures, Zurich, June, 1939–March, 1940; privately printed).
147. Jung, "The Process of Individuation," p. 24.
148. Cf. Jung, "Brother Klaus," *Psychology and Religion (CW 11).*
149. Freud has already rightly expressed regret that Descartes's associations, needful for a *certain* interpretation, are lacking—which is particularly the case with these human figures.
150. *A-T,* vol. 10, p. 186: "Il ajoute que le Génie qui excitait en luy l'enthousiasme dont il se sentait le cerveau échauffé depuis quelques jours, luy avoit prédit ce songe avant que de se mettre au lit et que l'esprit humain n'y avoit aucune part." ("He adds that the spirit which had excited in him the enthusiasm by which he had felt for several days that his brain was being heated, had predicted the dream to him before he went to bed, and that the human mind had no part in it.")
151. Cf. Sirven, pp. 131–132.
152. Adam, p. 305, and *A-T,* vol. 10, p. 213 (*Cogitationes privatae*): "Ut comoedi, moniti ne in fronte appareat pudor, personam induunt, sic ego, hoc mundi theatrum conscensurus, in quo hactenus spectator exstiti larvatus *prodeo.*" ("Just as comedians, warned that shame may appear on the

face, put on a mask, so I go forth masked when I am to
go into the theater of the world, in which until now I was
only a spectator.")
153. J. O. Wisdom interprets the school as "mother" in the
typical Freudian personalistic sense, although the Church,
as well as the school, probably held a maternal significance
in the wider meaning of the word for Descartes.
154. Cf. Adam, p. 22. For details of the school curriculum and
Descartes's teachers see Sirven (pp. 27ff., 31ff.), who notes
that Aristotle and Thomas Aquinas, in particular, were
studied extensively. Sirven stresses (pp. 31ff.): "Nous sais-
issons ainsi sur le vif l'interaction des diverses influences
qui se sont exercées sur son [Descartes's] esprit et que nous
sommes obligés de séparer pour rendre notre exposé plus
précis. Mais *l'idée primitive qui l'a orienté dans ce sens* [of an
intellectual discipline of thought] *lui est venue de la logique
de l'Ecole dont il a simplifié peut-être à l'excès les directions
générales*" (my italics). ("Thus we grasp the essence of the
interaction of the diverse influences that were exercised
over his [Descartes's] mind and that we are obliged to
separate in order to add precision to our *exposé*. But the
first primitive idea that oriented him in this direction [of
an intellectual mental discipline] came to him from Scholastic logic, the general instructions of which he simplified,
perhaps to excess.")
155. P. 86. Cf. also the additional literature there cited concerning this problem.
156. Cf. Celsius, *Hierobotan.* 1.356 and 2.47.
157. Numbers 11:5–6.
158. For the material see M.-L. von Franz, "The 'Passio Perpe-
tuae,' " *Spring* (New York: Analytical Psychology Club of
New York, Inc., 1949).
159. Pollux on Athen. 6.46C.
160. Pliny *Nat. hist.* 19.67.
161. See Pauly-Wissowa, *Realencycl. des Altertums, s.v.* "Me-
lone."
162. Pliny *Nat. Hist.* 21.6: "caro peponis mirifice refrigerat"
("flesh of melon is wonderfully [refreshing] cooling"). It is
considered to be particulary ὑγρός ("damp").
163. See O. von Hovorka and A. Kronfeld, *Vergleichende Volks-
medizin* (Stuttgart, 1909), vol. 2, p. 34.

164. *The I Ching, or Book of Changes,* trans. Cary F. Baynes from Richard Wilhelm's German ed.; 3d ed. (Princeton, N.J.: Princeton University Press, 1967), vol. 1, no. 44, "Coming to Meet." In regard to "nine in the fifth place" see vol. 2, p. 260.

165. A Spanish proverb also says of the melon: "Por la mañana oro / a mediodía plata / por la noche mata" ("In the morning gold, at midday silver, but at night death"). Another one says: "If you eat melon at night, even the neighbor feels sick."

166. *I Ching,* vol. 2, p. 257.

167. Cf. Jung, *Psychology and Alchemy,* pp. 71ff.

168. It is possible to compare this with the ghostly phenomena in Descartes's third dream, where this "subtle-body" quality of the psychic is also indicated.

169. Quoted from Jung, *Psychology and Alchemy,* pp. 71–72.

170. In *Japanische Volksmärchen,* ed. E. Diederichs (Jena, 1938), pp. 185ff. ("Die Märchen der Weltliteratur" series, ed. F. v. d. Leyen).

171. Cf. J. Bolte and G. Polivka, *Anmerkungen zu den Kinder- und Hausmärchen der Brüder Grimm* (Leipzig, 1912–32), vol. 4 (1930), p. 257, and the versions there given. Further variations may be found in vol. 2 (1915), p. 125.

172. Cf. A. Fischer, "Die Quitte als Vorzeichen bei Persern und Arabern und das Traumbuch des 'Abd-al-Ranī an-Nabulūsī," *Zeitschrift der deutschen morgenländischen Gesellschaft* 68 (Leipzig, 1914): 301, according to which quinces, lemons, pears, oranges, and "small melons" are frequently used poetic similes for women's breasts. Among the Persians the quince was a *"symbolum boni"* (p. 275) because it smells like musk, is gold-colored, and is shaped like a full moon (p. 300).

173. *Electi* = "high initiates."

174. See H. C. Puech, "Der Begriff der Erlösung im Manichäismus," *Eranos-Jahrbuch 1936* (Zurich, 1937), esp. pp. 258–259.

175. See *Acta Archelai,* ed. C. Beeson (Leipzig 1906), pp. 12–13, and Jung, *Psychology and Alchemy,* pp. 364–65.

176. See Puech, p. 259, and F. C. Baur, *Das manichäische Religionssystem* (Tübingen, 1831), esp. p. 287. Saint Augustine, *Contra Faustum* 5.10: "Si melioris meriti sunt (auditores) in

melones et cucumeres vel in alios aliquos cibos veniunt, quos vos mandacaturi estis, ut vestris ructatibus cito purgentur." ("If they [the hearers] are worthy of something better, they come to cucumbers, melons, and other foods which you will eat that *they* be quickly purged of your eructations.") Cf. also Baur, p. 250.

177. Cf. Baur, p. 250, viz., Augustine, *De moribus Manichaeorum*, chap. 16 (Migne, *Patr. Lat.*, vol. 32, col. 1362): "Cur de thesauris Dei melonem putatis aureum esse et pernae adipem rancidem? . . . [col. 1363:] An bona tria, ubi simul fuerint, i.e., color bonus et odor et sapor, ibi esse maiorem boni partem putatis?" ("Why do you consider, from the treasures of God, the melon gold, and the rancid fat of ham? . . . Do you think if these are good together, i.e., . . . good color, flavor, smell that there is the better part of good?") See, further, A. von le Coq, "Die buddhistische Spätantike in Mittelasien: Die manichäischen Miniaturen, II Teil," *Ergebnisse der kgl. preuss. TurfanExpedition* (Berlin: Reimer, 1923), where, on Plate 816, melons are depicted. As von le Coq realizes (p. 52), it concerns a representation of the so-called βῆμα festival in honor of the martyrdom of Mani in A.D. 273. This ceremony was solemnized in the presence of the empty tribune (βῆμα), the master's chair. The five steps that led up to it signified the five elements or grades—the Magistri, Episcopi, Presbyteres, Diaconi, and Electi. To the right and left were the sun and moon, for Mani is "medius Solis et Lunae" ("between the Sun and Moon"). In front of the tribune stood a bowl with three layers of fruit: at the bottom, yellow melons; in the middle, grapes; and on top, green melons. On the table lay wheat loaves in the shape of the sun's disk, with the sickle of the moon laid round it. I thank Jung for the reference to this material.

178. Cf. Sirven, pp. 145 ff. and esp. pp. 147–148. Descartes's definition of God as *"purus intellectus"* plainly stems from the treatise *De Genesi contra Manichaeos* (Sirven, p. 147).

179. For further details see below, p. 127.

180. Hippolytus *Elenchos* V. 19–22 (ed. P. Wendland; Leipzig, 1916); cf. also H. Leisegang, *Die Gnosis,* 2d ed. (Leipzig, 1924), pp. 151ff.

181. . . . γίνεται γὰρ τῶν δυνάμεων συνδρομὴ οἱονεί τις τύπος

σφραγῖδος (". . . for there is born from the powers a tumultuous concourse like some impression of a seal").

182. Αὗται οὖν εἰσιν αἱ εἰκόνες αἱ τῶν διαφόρων ζῴων ἰδέαι. ("These are the pictures, the 'ideal forms' of various living things.") The first collision makes the ἰδέα σφραγῖδος ("impress of seal") of heaven and earth and so forth. Expressed in modern language, these "seals" are the archetypes which engender the "images."

183. ἄνεμος σφοδρὸς καὶ λάβρος καὶ πάσης γενέσεως αἴτιος ("a keen, boisterious wind and the cause of all beginnings"). This may be compared with the storm in Descartes's dream.

184. σπινθὴρ ἐλάχιστος ("the least spark").

185. In that he drinks the "drink of living water" and lays aside the "form of the servant."

186. Irenaeus *Haer.* chap. 30; cf. also Leisegang, pp. 174ff.

187. Leisegang, p. 183.

188. Epiphanius *Panar.* 25–26; cf. also Leisegang, pp. 186ff.

189. Leisegang, pp. 189–190.

190. *Panar.* 26.3.1.

191. Leisegang, p. 195.

192. Ibid., pp. 196ff.

193. Ibid., pp. 215ff.

194. Ibid., pp. 218ff.

195. Cf. Jung, *Aion,* p. 80.

196. *Thesaurus* also means "treasure house, treasure chest."

197. For this term see Jung, *Psychology and Alchemy,* p. 42, and more especially "Concerning Mandala Symbolism," *The Archetypes and the Collective Unconscious,* p. 355 and passim.

198. Cf. *Psychology and Alchemy,* pp. 41–42.

199. Jung, *Paracelsica,* pp. 116–18.

200. Ibid., pp. 116ff.

201. Remember that he wanted to write a book called "Le Monde," in which he wished to draw up a complete picture of the macrocosmos.

202. *CW* 13.

203. An old alchemical text quoted ibid.

204. Ibid., p. 416, with further examples.

205. Ibid., pp. 418–20.

206. Quoted ibid., p. 421, with further examples.

207. My note: Cf. also the cabalistic Tree of Life, which grows

from above downward and which, as S. Hurwitz has informed me, is identified with *Adam Kadmon.*

208. Ibid., p. 422.

209. "Seminar über die psychologische Interpretation von Kinderträumen 1931–40," pp. 18–19. Quoted from the privately printed edition with the kind permission of C. G. Jung.

210. Cf. the example in *Psychology and Alchemy,* pp. 176–177.

211. Quoted from C. G. Jung and C. Kerényi, *Introduction to a Science of Mythology* (London: Routledge & Kegan Paul, 1951), p. 125.

212. Cf., among others, von Brockdorff, pp. 48–49, and S. Gagnebin, p. 117.

213. *A-T,* vol. 10, p. 33. In this same passage he also says: "Habet enim humana mens nescio quid divini, in quo cogitationum utilium semina iacta sunt." ("For the human mind possesses something divine in which the seeds of useful thoughts are sown.") He also speaks of *"quaedam veritatum semina"* ("certain seeds of truth") *A-T,* vol. 10, p. 376) and, in the *Cogitationes privatae* (*A-T,* vol. 10, p. 217), of *"semina scientiae"* ("seeds of science"). Cf. also Laporte, pp. 116–117, and Gagnebin, p. 118.

214. *A-T,* vol. 10, p. 185 and n.

215. Or, as Wisdom (p. 16) very pertinently says, "a serene relation to mother-earth."

216. Concerning the "uniting" function of the symbol see Jung, *Psychological Types,* passim.

217. Cf. the "Aniada" in Paracelsus, which he calls "fruits and powers of Paradise and of the heavens, and also the Sacraments of the Christians" (Jung, *Paracelsica,* pp. 122–124).

218. For further details see Jung, *Aion,* passim, esp. p. 80.

219. Compare with this Descartes's "provisional" moral doctrine, which, according to him, consisted in the commandment "d'obéir aux lois et aux coutumes de son pays, retenant constamment le religion en laquelle il avait été instruit dès son enfance" ("to obey the laws and customs of his country, holding fast to the religion in which he had been brought up from infancy") (cited in Gagnebin, p. 108).

220. Virgil *Aeneid* 2. 690–695.

221. Ibid.

222. Cf. Sirven, p. 129. For this reason I think it correct, in contrast to Sirven, to call it a "mystical crisis" and a genuine religious experience. Maritain speaks of a "Pentecost of reason." But Sirven objects: "Then, again, since this mysticism ought to be a secular mysticism, *clearly related to the subconscious,* its source is in the inspiration of the poets. . . ." Psychologically, the dream should be analyzed as a phenomenon of the unconscious only, without going into the problem of whether God is, in the final analysis, behind it, which cannot be established scientifically!

223. Jung, "A Study in the Process of Individuation," *The Archetypes and the Collective Unconscious,* pp. 295ff.

224. Cited ibid., p. 295, n.7. Cf. also Jung, *Paracelsica,* pp. 118–119.

225. Jung, "A Study in the Process of Individuation," p. 296.

226. Ibid.

227. Ibid.

228. Ibid., p. 295.

229. *Paracelsica,* p. 118.

230. Ibid., pp. 118–119.

231. "The Unconscious as a Multiple Consciousness," section 6 of "On the Nature of the Psyche," pp. 190ff.

232. Ibid., p. 189.

233. *Aurora Consurgens. 2: Artis Auriferae . . .* (1593), 1, 208 (quotation from Morienus, cited by Jung, ibid., p. 190, n. 54).

234. H. Khunrath, *Amphitheatrum* (1604), pp. 195, 198: "Variae eius radii atque Scintillae, per totius ingentem materiei primae massae molem hinc inde dispersae ac dissipatae; inque mundi partibus disiunctis etiam et loco et corporis mole, necnon circumscriptione, postea separatis . . . unius Animae universalis scintillae nunc etiam habitantes." ("The various rays and sparks in the huge mass of all matter in the first lump are [now] dispersed and scattered into the disjunct parts of the world which were later separated by mass and boundaries . . . which even today constitute the sparks of *one* universal world soul." (Cited by Jung, ibid., n. 55).

235. *Amphitheatrum,* p. 63 (cited by Jung, ibid., p. 191, n. 57): "Mens humani animi scintilla altior et lucidior." ("The

mind of the human spirit is a higher and more lucid spark.")

236. *Amphitheatrum*, p. 197 (cited by Jung, ibid.).
237. *Von hylealischen Chaos* (1597), p. 216 (cited by Jung, ibid.).
238. Paracelsus, *Philosophia sagax* (cf. Jung, ibid., p. 191).
239. *Paracelsus . . . Sämtliche Werke* (ed. Karl Sudhoff and Wilhelm Matthiessen) (Munich: Otto W. Barth, 1922–32), (cited by Jung, ibid., p. 193).
240. Cited by Jung, ibid., p. 194, from *Paracelsus . . . Sämtliche Werke,* vol. 13, p. 325.
241. Cited by Jung, ibid., p. 195, from *Paracelsus . . . Sämtliche Werke,* vol. 12, p. 53.
242. "Thus little by little he will come to see with his mental eyes a number of sparks shining day by day and more and more and growing into such a great light . . ." ("De speculativa philosophia," *Theati. Chem.* [1602], 1, 275; cited by Jung, ibid., p. 192).
243. See Jung, ibid., p. 195.
244. *De occulta philosophia* (Cologne, 1533), p. 48. (Cited by Jung, ibid., p. 195. Cf. also, ibid., Jung's further researches concerning the history of this conception of the *"sensus naturae";* see also his *Paracelsica* for the early alchemical history of the idea.)
245. Jung, "The Unconscious as a Multiple Consciousness," pp. 191, 192, 195.
246. Ibid., p. 192.
247. Ibid.
248. Ibid., p. 193.
249. Ibid., pp. 196 ff.
250. Ibid., p. 199.
251. In *The International Journal of Psycho-Analysis* 20 (1939): 43ff. Schönenberger's article is not given further consideration here because the author bases practically all his interpretations on quotations from Descartes's writings rather than on the dream motifs.
252. Especially in the *Discours* (*A-T,* vol. 6, pp. 44–45), where he speaks of the transformation of ashes into glass.
253. See Schönenberger and *A-T,* vol. 6, p. 26.
254. In a letter to Elizabeth von der Pfalz, 21 May 1643 (*A-T,* vol. 3, p. 665), Descartes says: ". . . je considère qu'il y a en nous certaines notions primitives qui sont comme des

originaux sur le patron desquels nous formons toutes nos autres connoissances. Et il n'y a que fort peu de telles notions; car après les plus générales de l'estre, du nombre, de la durée etc. qui conviennent à tout ce que nous pouvons concevoir; nous n'avons pour le corps en particulier que la notion de l'extension, de laquelle suivera celle de la figure et du mouvement, et pour l'âme nous n'avons que celle de la pensée, en laquelle sont comprises les perceptions de l'entendement et les inclinations de la volonté, enfin, pour l'âme et le corps ensemble nous n'avons que celle de leur union, de laquelle dépend celle de la force de l'âme de mouvoir le corps, et le corps d'agir sur l'âme en causant ses sentiments et ses passions." (". . . I consider that there are certain primitive ideas in us, which are like the patterns upon which we form all our other knowledge. And there are but very few of these ideas, for after the most general ones of being, number, duration, etc., which agree with everything of which we can conceive, for the body in particular, we have nothing but the idea of extension, from which will follow that of form and of movement, while for the soul we have only that of thought, in which are included the perceptions of understanding and the inclinations of the will; and finally, for the soul and body together we have only that of their union, on which depends the idea of the power of the soul to move the body, and of the body to act upon the soul by causing its feelings and its passions.") It is indicative of Descartes's type to equate feelings with bodily reactions and to look on them as secondary.

255. Quoted from the translation of E. Cassirer, Descartes's *Kritik der mathematischen und naturwissenschaftlichen Erkenntnis* (Marburg, 1899), p. 3.

256. Cf. also Barth, p. 12. Cf., further, the important part played by the image of the sun in Kepler's view of the world. See also W. Pauli, op. cit.

257. The Stoic doctrine of the *igniculi* or σπινθῆρες as the simplest elements of human reactions was known to him from Justus-Lipsius, *Manuductio ad philos. stoic.* Part 1, book 2, diss. 2 (1st ed., p. 72); cited in Gilson, p. 481, n. 2: "Igniculi isti non aliud quam inclinationes, judicia, et ex iis notiones sunt, a recta in nobis Ratione. Scito enim Stoicis

placere partem in nobis divini spiritus esse mersam, id est illam ipsam Rationem, quae si in suo loco et luce luceat, tota pura sincera, recta divina sit; nunc corpore velut carcere clausa, coercetur et opinionibus agitatur aut abducitur, et tamen retinet originis suae *flammulas* et Verum Honestumque per se et sua indole videt. Istae flammulae, sive igniculos mavis dicere Graeci σπινθῆρας, ζώπυρα, ἐναύσματα appellant exserunt se et ostendunt in sensibus aut judiciis, quae omni hominum generi fere, et optimae cuique naturae eximie sunt insita aut innata. Id Graeci Ἐννοίας sive Notiones vocant item προλήψεις *Anticipationes* et quia passivae atque insitae κοινὰς καὶ ἐμφύτας communes et ingeneratas agnominarunt." ("These sparks are nothing but inclinations, judgmentᵉ. From them come notions, by right reasoning within ս̣s. Because the Stoics liked to call that part lodged in us the spirit of the divine, i.e., that very reason which, when placed and shining in its own place, is pure, sincere, whole, and justly divine; now in the body as if shut in a prison, it is coerced, led astray, and agitated by opinions, and yet it retains the little flames of its origins and sees the true and honest by itself and its inborn quality. These little flames—or you may prefer to call them little fires [the Greeks call them 'sparks; life-giving sparks']—poke out and show feelings and judgments. These are innate in almost every sort of human and are excellently placed in the best natures. These the Greeks call 'reflections, conceptions, or notions.' Likewise they call them 'preconceptions, anticipations.' And because they are passive and placed there, they call them 'common and inborn.' ") As Gilson emphasizes (ibid., n. 3), Descartes's phrase *bona mens* can probably also be traced back to the same work (*Manuductio,* pp. 70–71), where it says: "Ecce Natura bonae Mentis nobis ingenuit *fomites et scintillas,* quae in aliis magis minusque elucent." Cf. also P. Gibieuf, *De libertate Dei et creaturae* (Paris, 1630), 1,1: "Primae et universalissimae rerum qualitatumque notiones non concinnantur hominum arte et industria, nec ad arbitrium etiam philosophorum effinguntur, sed in mentibus nostris reperiuntur a natura consignatae. Qui autem animo ad tranquillitatem composito naturam audiunt, vel si paulo dignius loqui mavis, qui veritatem intus presidentem et responsa dantem consiliunt [must mean: 'consulunt'] illas tamquam in alto puteo delitescentes percipiunt." ("First and most universal notions of things and qualities are not constituted by the art and industry of men. They are not fashioned by the arbitrary judgment of philosophers but are set in our minds by nature—they are discovered there. Moreover, whoever listens to nature with a mind kept tranquil—or to put it in a little less dignified way, whoever proceeds to the truth that presides within and gives answers—will catch sight of them as if they were hidden in a deep well.")

258. For further details see *A-T*, vol. 10, pt. 1, p. 183, n. Cf. Stock, pp. 60 ff.

259. For further details concerning this publication see *A-T*, vol. 10, p. 183, n.

260. Also worth noting is the connection with Wotan, who is related to storm, the spirits of the dead, and to *magic*.

261. For details cf. Stock, p. 11. God *cannot* deceive, neither can the thinking substance in us; at most it is our understanding that cheats.

262. Or a *"Sapientia generalis."* Cf. Regulae (*A-T*, vol. 10, pp. 360–361).

263. Cf. *A-T*, vol. 10, p. 383: "Notandum 2. paucas esse duntaxat *naturas puras et simplices,* quas primo et per se, non dependenter ab aliis ullis, sed vel in ipsis experimentis *vel lumine quodam in nobis insito* licet intueri . . ." ("Second to be noted: [Such] pure and simple natures are not really very many. Firstly they are to be seen only through themselves, or in experiences, or by a certain light placed in us.") And, ibid., p. 419: "Purae intellectuales illae (*scil.* res) sunt, quae per lumen quoddam ingenitum et absque ullius imaginis corporeae adiumento ab intellectu cognoscuntur. . . ." ("Those things are purely intellectual which are learned by the intellect through a certain inborn light without the aid of any corporeal form.")

264. *Meditation 3* (*A-T*, vol. 9, p. 33). For this reason Leibniz (*Philosophische Schriften*, ed. G. L. Gehrhardt [Hildesheim: Olms, 1960], vol. 4, pp. 328, 371), criticizes: "veritatis criterium nihil aliud esse quam visionem" ("the criterion of truth being nothing but a vision"). Cf. Laporte, p. 21, n. 1.

265. *Meditation* 5. Cf. Laporte, pp. 116, 117.
266. "Recherche de la vérité par la lumière naturelle" (*A-T,* vol. 10, p. 527; cf. also p. 495).
267. Cf. Laporte, p. 319: "L'ensemble des idées distinctes dont se compose notre raison est littéralement non pas une 'vision en Dieu' (Descartes ne dit rien de tel mais une *révélation naturelle que Dieu nous fait).*" ("The harmony of the separate ideas of which our reason is composed is quite literally not a 'vision in God' [Descartes says nothing of the kind, but a natural revelation that God grants to us].") Cf. Karl Löwith, "Das Verhältnis von Gott, Mensch und Welt in der Metaphysik von Descartes und Kant," *Sitzungsberichte der Heidelberger Akad. der Wiss., Phil.-hist. Klasse* (1964), transaction 3.
268. Goethe revolted with feeling agairʒt this one-sidedness: "He [Descartes] makes use of the crudest sensory similes in order to explain the impalpable, indeed the inconceivable. His various material examples, his vortices, his screws, hooks, and pointed curves, thus drag the spirit down. When ideas of this sort are accepted with approval, then it shows that just the rawest, clumsiest views harmonize with the general outlook." Quoted from Fleckenstein, p. 124.
269. Wisdom (p. 14) says that Descartes laid these realizations aside and then took them up again. But in the dream it is *not* Descartes who does this. "It" conjures the books from here and there.
270. For material see Stock, p. 10.
271. God is *"intelligentia pura"* ("pure intelligence"); see *Cogitationes privatae* (*A-T,* vol. 10, p. 218).
272. See von Brockdorff, p. 36, and *Regulae* (*A-T,* vol. 10, p. 368): "Per intuitum intelligo non *fluctuantem sensuum fidem* vel male componentis imaginationis iudicium fallax; sed mentis purae et attentae tam facilem distinctumque conceptum, ut de eo, quod intelligimus nulla prorsus dubitatio relinquatur." ("By intuition I mean not our wavering trust in our senses nor the fallible judgment of a disorderly imagination, but the easy and clear distinctions of a purified and attentive mind so that no further doubt remains about what we understand.") Concerning his doctrine of sensory perception through *"phantasmata"* see Gilson, pp. 470ff.

273. Felsch, p. 19, and esp. pp. 44ff., 49.
274. Ibid., p. 49.
275. Ibid., p. 50.
276. Ibid., p. 50–51.
277. Ibid., p. 53.
278. That this was the case, see Sirven, pp. 146ff.
279. *CW* 9, part II.
280. See *A-T,* vol. 10, p. 218.
281. See ibid., p. 146.
282. Migne, *Patr. Lat.,* 34, col. 229.
283. Ibid., col. 176, and 41, cols. 332–33.
284. Sirven, pp. 147–148.
285. Cf. ibid., p. 149.
286. Cf. Laporte, p. 171, where he shows that Descartes deduces the veracity of God from the fact that God cannot introduce any nonbeing into his being: "Mais le mot 'tromper' n'a pas de sens où il signifie le substitution du faux au vrai. En faisant de la tromperie un bien Dieu introduirait en soi du non-être: ce qui reviendrait à s'ôter un peu de son être. . . ." ("But the word 'to deceive' has no sense where it means the substitution of the false for the true. By committing deceit, a good 'God' would introduce into himself some nonbeing: which would amount to removing a little of himself. . . ."
287. Maritain, p. 41: "mesurant la terre et trouvant tout droit Dieu dans l'âme."
288. Ibid., p. 55: "brise . . . en deux morceaux contrastant, qu'elle affirme chacun à part sans pouvoir désormais les réunir, les conciliations supérieures, en lesquelle la scolastique resolvait les grandes antinomies de réel. . . ."
289. "The Phenomenology of the Spirit in Fairy Tales," *The Archetypes and the Collective Unconscious,* pp. 234–235.
290. The three-headed Satan, and so forth. In folklore a similar triad also often appears, for Satan is given a "grandmother" and a beautiful daughter with "human" feelings.
291. Ibid., pp. 251–252.
292. Brunschvicg, pp. 117–118: "Une physique où le mécanisme est pratiqué avec autant de rigueur et dans une semblable extension ne risque-t-elle pas de frayer la voie à la renaissance du matérialisme épicurien? . . . mais tout au contraire, parce que la manière dont il introduit et justifie

la vérité du mécanisme intégral, immanent en quelque
sorte à lui-même, *plonge ses racines dans une métaphysique
dont on ne doit pas dire seulement, qu'elle est radicalement
spiritualiste, mais qui renouvelle, en la portant à un degré de
pureté jusqu'alors insoupçonné, la notion de spiritualité.*"
("Does not a physics where the mechanism is practiced
with as much rigor and to such an extent risk opening up
the road to a rebirth of Epicurean materialism . . . ? But
quite the contrary! Because the manner in which it introduces and justifies the truth of the integral mechanism,
immanent in some way in itself, *plunges its roots into a
metaphysics of which one not only ought to say that it is radically
spiritual but that it even renews, by bringing to it a degree of
purity unsuspected up to now, the notion of spirituality.*") This
"abstraction" is grounded in the geometric nature of Descartes's physics. Cf. Gagnebin, p. 117.

293. Cf. Stock, pp. 75ff. Descartes hypostasizes space as absolutely existent; cf. Gagnebin, p. 116: "la géométrie de
Descartes est déjà une physique" ("Descartes's geometry
is already a physics").

294. Cf. Stock, p. 49, and Gagnebin, p. 116.

295. Concerning Descartes's "sceptique chrétienne" see Adam,
p. 57. It might perhaps be still more important to stress
that Descartes really only thought about an intellectual
solution to the moral problem and did not look on moral-
ity as a concern of the feeling-function.

296. "The proverb of the Greeks is the best: they say it is best
for man not to be born or to die soon."

297. Descartes himself calls it "le bon conseil d'une personne
sage ou même la Théologie Morale" ("the good counsel
of a wise person or even of Moral Theology").

298. In the history of religion this is the name specially given to
the divine savior-figures in many American Indian tribes,
because they are particularly noted for their queer, elfish
tricks. The alchemistic Spirit Mercurius is likewise fond of
appearing as a "trickster."

299. For the text and translation of this poem, see below, pp.
140f.

300. Wisdom (p. 14) also stresses this point: ". . . the anthology
meant the knowledge of what is real in the life of the
living."

301. In the "Recherche de la vérité" (*A-T,* vol. 10, p. 507) Descartes speaks of the deceptions of the senses as being inferior pictures, painted by apprentice artists, to which the master (Reason) puts finishing touches. But according to Descartes, the master would do better to start from the beginning again.

302. Jung, *Paracelsica,* p. 116. Concerning the *Multiplicatio* cf. Jung, "The Psychology of the Transference," *The Practice of Psychotherapy* (*CW* 16), pp. 304ff., and for the Self as the condition of relatedness see ibid., pp. 233ff.

303. *A-T,* vol. 10, p. 185; Sirven, p. 129.

304. Cf. J. H. Gouhier: "Le refus du symbolisme dans l'humanisme cartésien," *Umanismo e simbolismo: Atti del VI convegno internat. di studi umanistici* (Padua, 1958), p. 67, and Rossi, pp. 154ff.

305. This is a typical phenomenon, that is, that people suffering from feelings of inferiority do not connect them with their actually inferior side but shift them to a side where they have no need to feel so inferior.

306. Cf. *A-T,* vol. 10, p. 180, where A. Baillet remarks, concerning his condition before the dream: "Avec toutes ces dispositions il n'eut pas moins à souffrir que s'il eût été question de se dépouiller de soy-même. Il crût pourtant en être venu à bout. Et à dire vrai, c'étoit assez que son imagination *lui representât son esprit tout nud,* pour lui faire croire qu'il l'avoit mis effectivement en cet état. Il ne lui restoit que l'amour de la vérité dont la poursuite devoit faire dorénavant l'occupation de sa vie." ("With all those preparations, he suffered no less than if it had been a matter of stripping himself of himself. He thought, however, that he had reached the end. And truth to tell, it was enough that his imagination should show him his mind entirely naked, to make him believe that he had in fact reduced it to that condition. Nothing remained for him but the love of truth, the pursuit of which was to be the occupation of his life from that time on.")

307. *Confinia psychiatrica* 4 (1961), passim.

GLOSSARY

Alchemy The chemistry from prehistory until the seventeenth century, in which laboratory experiments were combined with intuitive, pictorial, partly religious experiences about nature and man. Many symbols which we recognize today as contents of the unconscious were projected onto matter, onto the *prima materia* (q.v.). The alchemist sought the "secret of God" in the primary material and, in doing so, developed methods and processes which resemble those of modern depth psychology.

Alter ego (Latin) The other aspect of oneself, a second ego; also, one's doppelgänger.

Amplification Expansion of the dream content through personal associations and comparison of the dream images with images from mythology, religion, and so on, which resemble the dream content.

Anima Personification of the feminine nature in the unconscious of a man; the contrasexual soul image, the image of *the* feminine which is internalized in the male psyche.

Animus Personification of the masculine nature in the unconscious of a woman. The animus is often recognized in projection onto spiritual authorities; in this way, a woman's inner image of masculinity finds expression.

Apocrypha Scriptural works which have not been acknowledged as a part of the canon (q.v.) but which are similar in form and content to the accepted biblical texts.

Archetypes Structural elements or dominants in the psyche which are in themselves indescribable, but which express themselves as dream and fantasy images and as fantasy motifs in consciousness; primordial images.

Behaviorism School of psychology that limits itself to the objectively observable and to measurable behavior, dispensing with any description of the contents of consciousness which emerge only by way of introspection.

Canon Scriptural texts officially accepted by a church as authentic and immutable.

Collective unconscious The deeper levels of the unconscious, which Jung recognizes as containing the totality of all archetypes which reflect experiences common to all men. The forms of the archetypal structures (not their content) are hereditary and are comparable to the inborn behavior patterns of animals, such as nest building, bee dancing, courtship, and so forth.

Compensation Counterbalance; in a psychological sense, the appearance of an opposite attitude in behavior which is too one-sided.

Complementarity Completion; psychologically, the assimilation of an element which has previously been lacking and through which wholeness is attained.

Coniunctio (Latin) Union, connection by love.

Constellation A time-bound grouping of events.

Daimon Originally a value-free, driving force, a spiritual energy which leads to the creative formation of individuality; for Socrates, an inspiring and guiding spirit.

Demiurge (Greek-Latin) The artisan of the universe, creator of all the worlds (especially in Plato and the Gnostics).

Djinn Supernatural spirit, Arabic for "demon."

Extraversion, extraverted Directed outwardly. A psychic attitude, characterized by a concentration of interest on objects; easily susceptible to outer influences.

Heretic (Greek-Latin) One who deviates from official Church dogma.

Individuation "Individuation means becoming an 'in-dividual,' and, insofar as 'individuality' embraces our innermost, last, and incomparable uniqueness, it also implies becoming one's own self."—C. G. Jung, *Two Essays on Analytical Psychology,* par. 266.

Inferior function In Jung's typology, that function of the four functions of behavior (thinking, feeling, sensation, intuition) which has not been developed and hence has remained inferior. It is the opposite of the strongest or superior function (for instance, with a thinking personality feeling is usually less developed).

Inflation An overexpansion of the personality through identification with an archetype or, in pathological cases, with a historical or religious figure, which exceeds individual limitations.

Introversion, introverted Directed inwardly; a concentration of energy on inner-psychic processes, oriented to an inner evaluation of experience.

Katoche (Greek) Confinement, imprisonment; also, to be in the power of a god, or possession.

Libido (Latin, "desire," "love") In Jung's terminology, the psychic energy that underlies all psychic manifestations (drives, aspirations, etc.).

Logos (Greek-Latin) Meaningful word, logical decision or judgment, human intellect; divine reason, world reason, God's Word as the force which created the world; revelation.

Lysis (Greek) In dream theory, the resolution or ending events of the dream.

Mandala (Sanskrit) Literally "circle." An image inserted in a circle or polygon which facilitates meditation and is intended to represent certain spiritual dynamics. Mandalas are widespread in most religious traditions. In Jung's psychology they are recognized as unconscious contents which emerge into consciousness spontaneously and serve as symbols of the totality of the personality or of the Self.

Objective level A type of dream interpretation in which persons and objects appearing in the dream are understood as having objective meaning. In such an interpretation one is concerned with the relation between the dreamer and the environment. (See also *Subjective level*.)

Participation mystique   A psychological condition in which various inanimate objects and people participate with each other in a mystical manner, are connected with each other beneath the surface of consciousness. The French philosopher and sociologist Lucien Lévy-Bruhl coined this expression for the characteristic of a possible identification of all things with each other, especially observable in children and primitives.

Pneuma   (Greek) Breath. An airlike substance believed to be a dynamic principle.

Prima materia   In alchemy the primary matter which has not yet been transformed.

Privatio boni   (Latin) Literally, "absence of good." A doctrine of the Roman Catholic Church (Basil the Great, Dionysius the Aeropagite, Saint Augustine) according to which evil is merely a "diminished good" and does not exist per se.

Psychoid   Psyche-like, quasi-psychic. For Jung, characteristic of the unobservable deep layer of the collective unconscious and its contents.

Psychopomp   (Greek, *pompos,* companion, escort, messenger) In mythology, a guide who conducts departed souls to the underworld; in psychology, the "soul guide."

Self   Center and circumference of the total psyche, that is, the conscious and unconscious personality of man.

Shadow   In analytical psychology, the neglected qualities of the personality in the conscious process of integration, consisting of partly repressed, partly unlived traits which, for social, ethical, educational, or other reasons, have been excluded from conscious experience and therefore have fallen into the unconscious. The shadow is in a compensatory relation to consciousness; it can therefore function positively as well as negatively.

Subjective level   A specific method of dream interpretation in which figures and situations that appear in the dream are interpreted as partial aspects of the dreamer himself. The subjective level of interpretation is concerned with the relation of the dreamer to his inner world. (See also *Objective level*.)

Synchronicity A concept coined by Jung. It denotes a meaningful coincidence or correspondence of two or more outer and inner events. It signifies the meaningful concurrence of a physical and a psychic event which are connected not causally but by meaning.

Tao (Chinese) Usually translated as "way," "universal meaning," "World Ground." That which keeps the world meaningfully together in its innermost parts.

Theriomorphic (Greek) Animal-shaped.

Typology A model of classification based on the predominance of psychic activity of certain distinct ways of understanding and perceiving; for Jung, it is connected with the two attitudes, namely extraversion and introversion, and the four functions: thinking, feeling, sensation, intuition. For example, a thinking type experiences the world and attempts to understand it through his thinking function which is more highly developed than his other functions. Cf. C. G. Jung, *Psychological Types*.

C. G. JUNG FOUNDATION BOOKS